AF618476

THE EPIC
POLA SIEVERDING

HATJE
CANTZ

ARENA UND THE EPIC. ZUR PRODUKTION VON NICHT-EVIDENZ

KIRSTEN MAAR

ARENA AND THE EPIC: ON THE PRODUCTION OF NON-EVIDENCE

KIRSTEN MAAR

In *Arena* sehen wir die Körper von Männern in Wrestling-Montur – die Oberfläche der glänzenden Haut, die leuchtende Farbigkeit der Monturen und den starken Kontrast vor dem schwarzen Hintergrund, der bereits deutlich macht, dass es sich um eine Inszenierung handelt. Sie erinnern an Rubens' bewegte Fleischmassen, nur dass die Körper hier durchaus trainiert sind, sie evozieren die sportlichen Wettkämpfe der Antike, obwohl es keine asketischen Sportler oder athletischen Typen sind. Der Kontext, auch wenn er durch den schwarzen Hintergrund weitestgehend ausgeblendet ist, ähnelt auf den ersten Blick den Inszenierungen von Boxkämpfen. Vielleicht denkt man auch an die traurig-tragische Figur, die Mickey Rourke als alternder Wrestler in Darren Aronofskys Film aus dem Jahr 2008 abgibt, der eine Welt des ambivalenten Glamours eröffnet.

Beim Wrestling steht nicht allein der sportliche Wettkampf im Mittelpunkt, sondern zugleich auch dessen Inszenierung, das Theatrale des Wettkampfs, das die Kämpfenden in einen bestimmten Kontext versetzt, in ein spezifisches Licht rückt. Das Betreten einer Bühne, das Licht der Scheinwerfer, der Moment des Erscheinens vor dem Publikum machen aus dem Kampf eine Art Galavorstellung und die Wrestler zu den Diven des Rings: verletzbar und doch mit einem spezifisch männlich konnotierten Habitus der scheinbaren Unbesiegbarkeit. Es geht um alles in jedem Kampf, der zugleich auch eine große Show ist, aufgeladen mit hohem affektiven Potenzial. Nicht umsonst daher die leuchtenden Farben der Wrestling-Monturen, die innerhalb eines codierten Rituals Stärke, Macht und Attraktivität suggerieren.

Unterstrichen wird dieses Auftreten durch Haltungen, durch einen spezifischen Habitus, der sich wiederum deutlich vom Habitus des Boxens oder Ringens unterscheidet. Die Körperhaltungen, die durchaus als inszenierte Posen erscheinen, lassen jedoch zugleich den Verlauf einer Bewegung antizipieren, denn Pola Sieverding fängt die Bewegung der Männer meist im Clinch ein, wenn sich die Kämpfer ineinander verschlungen zwischen Besiegen und Umklammerung mit- und gegeneinander bewegen. Die Unentschiedenheit dieser Situation ist es, die die Bilder mit einer Spannung auflädt, die mehr als diesen Moment umfängt.

Die Körperbilder – oder vielmehr die Körperinszenierungen – materialisieren sich im Helldunkel der Kontraste, sie werden durch das Spiel des Lichts auf der Haut

In *Arena,* we see the bodies of men in wrestling regalia: the shiny surface of the skin, the glowing colors of the regalia and the strong contrast against the black background that makes the staging clear from the outset. The bodies call to mind Rubens' mobile masses of flesh, except these bodies are highly trained, evoking, though these are not ascetic sportsmen or athletic types, the sporting competitions of classical antiquity. The context, though almost entirely masked out by the black background, at first resembles the staging of boxing matches. Perhaps we are also reminded of the mournful and tragic figure Mickey Rourke plays of the aging wrestler in Darren Aronofsky's 2008 film, revealing a world of ambivalent glamour.

At wrestling's core is not only an athletic competition but also its staging and mise-en-scène, the theatricality of competition, putting the fighters in a certain context, placing them in a specific light. Going onstage, the spotlights, the moment of going in front of the audience turn the fight into a kind of gala event and the wrestlers into divas of the ring: vulnerable, yet with a specifically male-connotated habitus of apparent invincibility. Every fight is a fight for everything, and at the same time a big show, charged with high affective potential. It is not for nothing that wrestling regalia is in glowing colors, suggesting strength, power and attraction within a coded ritual. This performance is underscored by a set of postures, by a specific habitus, itself clearly different from the actual habitus of boxing and amateur wrestling.

The body postures, which appear as entirely staged poses, allow us to anticipate the course of a movement. Pola Sieverding for the most part captures the movement of the men in a clinch, when the fighters move with and against each other, mutually entangled between conquering and embracing. The indecisiveness of the situation is what charges the images with a tension that surrounds more than the moment.

The body images—or rather the body stagings—materialize in the chiaroscuro of contrasts. They are emphasized by the play of light on the skin that renders the musculature visible. The carnality of the bodies, tending to elude normative ideals of beauty, becomes the real event in the performance of the spectacle and the exhibition. Not the fight itself, but rather its visuality makes palpable in a moment the drama of conquering and being conquered.

hervorgehoben, durch das die Muskulatur sichtbar wird. Die Fleischlichkeit der Körper, die sich normativen Schönheitsidealen eher entzieht, wird in der Performanz der Aufführung und Ausstellung zu dem eigentlichen Ereignis. Nicht der Kampf selbst, sondern seine Bildlichkeit macht das Drama des Siegens oder Besiegtwerdens in einem Augenblick fassbar.

Medien, Unmittelbarkeit und Materialität

Bereits mit diesen Beschreibungen sind wir nicht mehr auf der Ebene des Unmittelbaren, sondern inmitten dessen, was den Kampf sowie seine Betrachtung durch uns auf verschiedenen medialen Ebenen strukturiert. Durch Körper- und Kampftechniken, die im Training erworben werden, mithilfe von Inszenierungsweisen, die von der Lichtregie bis hin zu den »Kostümen« und der fast rituellen Anordnung des Wrestling-Rings reichen, wird unser Blick gelenkt. Wie in den Arenen der Antike, aber auch im antiken Theater wird der Ring, die Bühne vom Publikum umschlossen und steht dadurch buchstäblich im Zentrum der Aufmerksamkeit. Außer durch diese der Situation immanenten Aspekte wird unser Blick aber auch durch die fotografische Perspektive gelenkt sowie durch die Entscheidung, die Szenen von ihrem situativen Kontext – nämlich jenem vielleicht vorhandenen Publikum beziehungsweise dem Trainingsraum – zu trennen, zu abstrahieren, um uns als Betrachter/-innen an deren Stelle treten zu lassen.

Die Rauminstallation in der Ausstellung *The Epic* im NAK Neuer Aachener Kunstverein (Abb. S. 17 ff.) nimmt ähnlich wie die Installation im Museum Abteiberg (Abb. S. 11) auf einer dritten Ebene Anordnungen vor, welche die verschiedenen Konstellationen zwischen den Wrestlern und zwischen ihnen und ihren Betrachter/-innen im Ausstellungsraum bestimmen – das neue Publikum quasi im Raum choreografieren. So wird der Kampf selbst zu einem Ereignis, das sich auf verschiedensten Ebenen und über unterschiedliche Medien, Verfahren und Techniken vermittelt – auch wenn es uns scheinbar unmittelbar ergreift.

Das Auffächern eines Registers von Anspielungen ist dem Geschehen immanent, und so ist es zeitlich stets sowohl auf die soeben vergangene Bewegung als auch auf eine fiktive Potenzialität hin ausgerichtet. Durch Wiederholung und Variation sich materialisierende Gesten, Posen, Bewegungen werden erst im Akt der

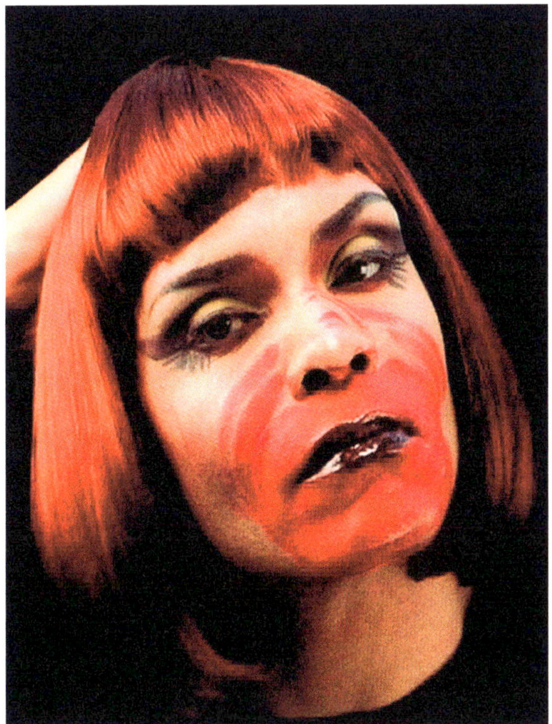

Media, Immediacy and Materiality

With these descriptions, we have already departed from the level of the immediate and are instead in the midst of those things that structure, on a variety of medial levels, both the fight as well as our observation of it. Our gaze is directed by body and fighting techniques gained through training, with the help of methods of staging from lighting design to the "costumes" and an almost ritual arrangement of the wrestling ring. As in the arenas and theaters of classical antiquity, the ring and the stage, since surrounded by the audience, are literally at the center of attention. Beyond these aspects inherent to the given situation, our gaze is also directed by the photographic perspective and by the decision to separate, to abstract the scenes from their given situation—namely the audience or the training room that may have been present—so as to let us replace them as observers.

The whole-room installation in the exhibition *The Epic* at NAK Neuer Aachener Kunstverein (ill. p. 17ff.), like the artist's installation at the Museum Abteiberg in Mönchengladbach (ill. p. 11), implements a third level of arrangements that determine the various configurations among the wrestlers and between the wrestlers and their

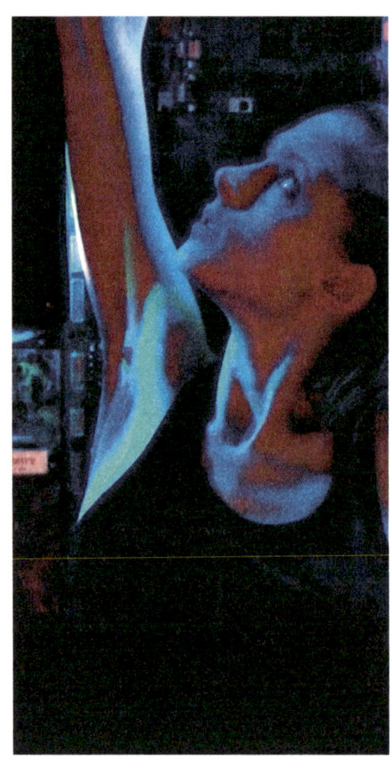
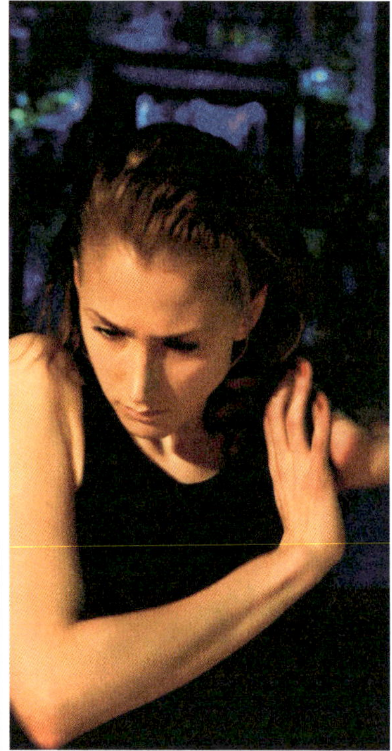
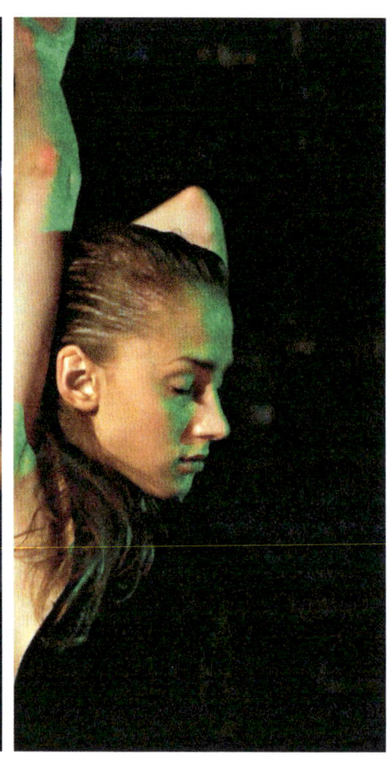
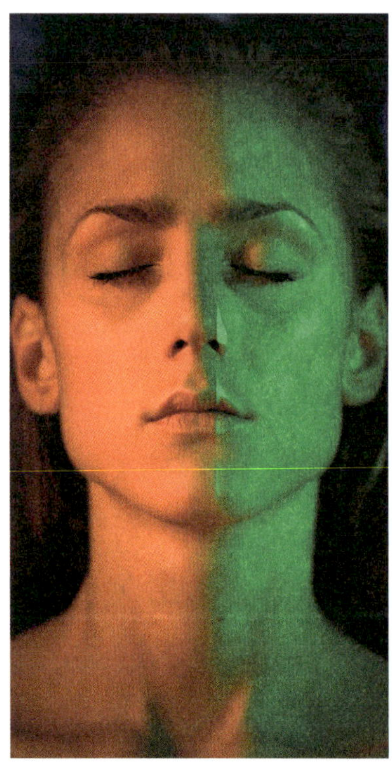
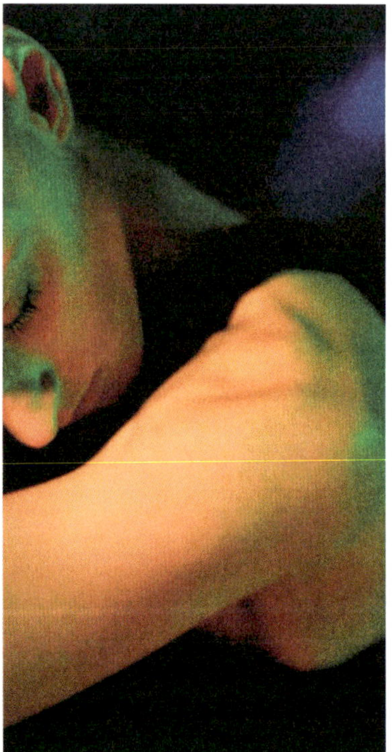
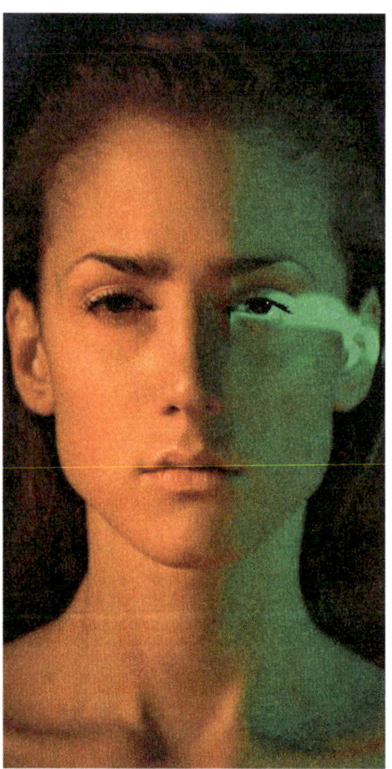

Betrachtung als ein in sich performatives Geschehen greifbar. Doch nicht nur die Antizipierbarkeit von Bewegungsverläufen, sondern auch das Situative und Kontextuelle dieser Anordnung von Bildern tragen dazu bei. Es sind die Bilder von Ähnlichem, die kleinen Verschiedenheiten der Körper, die Details, das »Beiwerk«, die Weiterentwicklung der Posen von Bild zu Bild, die uns die einzelnen Fotografien in einen größeren Zusammenhang stellen lassen – eine Art Bilderatlas, der die Ikonografie bestimmt. Die zahlreichen möglichen Verweise und Beziehungen, wie sie eingangs ansatzweise zitiert wurden, spannen den Akt der Betrachtung in ein Spiel zwischen Sichtbarem und Unsichtbarem ein.

The Epic – sowohl Titel der Ausstellung als auch Titel des gezeigten Films mit zwei Boxern – verweist auf das Epos, die große Erzählung und breite Darstellung eines monumentalen Heldennarrativs, die jedoch nicht nur aus Gründen der Rede von deren Ende in der Postmoderne, sondern vor allem ob ihrer immanenten Ambivalenz nur noch als mehrfach gebrochene erscheinen kann, eine Gebrochenheit, die sich auch in der räumlichen Anordnung spiegelt. Ebenso evoziert der Titel aber auch das epische Theater Brechts, das nicht einfach darstellt und die Zuschauer möglichst unmittelbar ergreift, sondern zugleich sichtbar macht, wie es darstellt, auf bestimmte Aspekte zeigt, sie hervorhebt, rahmt – und andere wiederum verschwinden lässt. Verfremdung erscheint hier als Detailverschiebung eines realistischen Blicks auf die Konstellationen von Alltag und Fiktionalisierung.

Im Spiel dieser verschiedenen Verweisebenen sind es vor allem die Materialität der Körper, die vor dem schwarzen Hintergrund erscheinen, die glänzende, schwitzende und geölte Haut der Wrestler, die Tattoos, die Qualität der Polyesterstoffe, die Geübtheit der Griffe und der Mimik, die der Dramatik im Verlauf des Kampfs das Moment der Ausdauer der Kämpfenden gegenüberstellen, den Schmerz, den Verschleiß der Körper, die Verausgabung. Verstärkt wird diese Wirkung durch Detailaufnahmen der Protagonisten, die einzelnen Partien in Bewegung, die den Körper fragmentieren und dessen Materialisierungen als Suche nach verschiedenen Identitäten ausgeben.

observers in the exhibition rooms, choreographing, as it were, the new audience in space. The fight becomes an event that communicates itself on a wide variety of levels and via different media, processes and techniques—even as it seems to reach us directly.

Unfolding a range of allusions is immanent to the event, and therefore temporally always oriented both to the movement that has just happened and to a fictive potentiality. It is through the act of observation that gestures, poses and movements that are materialized through repetition and variation first become tangible as events that are performative in and of themselves. Contributing to this tangibility is not only the fact that paths of movement can be anticipated, but also the situational nature and contextuality of this arrangement of images. These are images of similar things, of small differences in bodies, details, "accessories," the further development of individual poses. The differences are what allow us to place individual photographs in a larger context—a kind of photo atlas defining the iconography. The numerous possible references and relationships, a few of which have been mentioned above, insert the act of observation into a play between visible and invisible.

The Epic—the title both of the exhibition and of the film shown with two boxers—refers to the great narration and broad depiction of a monumental hero narrative, a narrative that today can appear only as multiply broken, given the discussion of the end of narratives in postmodernism and given, moreover, narratives' immanent ambivalence. This brokenness is reflected in the spatial layout as well. The title furthermore evokes Bertolt Brecht's epic theater, which does not merely represent and reach the observer as directly as possible, but at the same time makes visible *how* it represents, showing, emphasizing, framing certain aspects—and in turn making others disappear. Here alienation appears as a shifting of the details of a realistic gaze onto the configurations of everyday life and fictionalization.

In the play of these different levels of reference, the materiality of the bodies against the black background, the wrestlers' glistening, sweating, oiled skin, the tattoos, the quality of the polyester fabrics, the proficiency of the holds and the facial expressions all create a particular contrast, showing over the course of the fight, in counterpoint to the dramatics, the quantum of stamina the fighters have, their pain, the wearing out and burning out

Queering expectations

Dennoch sind es nicht wie in den früheren Arbeiten queere Körperinszenierungen, innerhalb derer Geschlechternormen oder Körperbilder verhandelt werden, eher geht es um ein *queering* dessen, was wir als Betrachter/-innen erwarten, ein Unterlaufen bestimmter normativer Vorstellungen. Denn es macht durchaus einen Unterschied, ob ein Mann, eine Frau, ob ein anderes Geschlecht sie betrachtet und was man in diesen Körperbildern wiederfindet oder finden will. Herkömmliche Definitionen wie *gender trouble* oder *queer performance* scheinen nicht zu passen, denn schon die vorangegangenen Arbeiten von Pola Sieverding stellen auch neue Genderkategorien bereits wieder infrage. In einer früheren Arbeit – *Make Up* (2010) (Abb. S. 7) – sehen wir die langsame Transformation vom Maskulinen ins Feminine. Die Szene: ein Schminktisch, vor dem aus einem Mann in einem langsamen Prozess der Verwandlung eine Diva wird – das Gesicht erscheint im Close-up, die Kamera fängt den Blick in der intimen Perspektive des Spiegels. Die Verwandlung kippt jedoch, als der Mund durch das Auftragen des Lippenstifts immer größer und größer wird, bis schließlich das ganze Gesicht signalrot leuchtet. Das Entfernen des Make-ups, die Dekonstruktion wird mit der gleichen Langsamkeit zelebriert wie der Prozess des Entstehens.

In einer anderen Arbeit, *Cross Metropolis Machine* (2012) (Abb. S. 8), die in der Installation im Museum Abteiberg in Mönchengladbach gemeinsam mit den Wrestlern und Boxern gezeigt wurde, sehen wir eine einzelne Clubtänzerin. Ihre filigranen Bewegungen der Finger und Arme scheinen zunächst ein gängiges Bild des Tanzes als Bewegung der schönen Form zu bestätigen, jedoch sucht sie stets neue Positionen, ihr Blick ist zwar direkt in die Kamera gerichtet, doch wirkt er tranceartig und in sich versunken. Im Zoom auf die einzelnen Partien des Körpers, die im Wechsel von Dunkel und farbigem Licht als abgetrennte, lebendige Materie erscheinen, nähert sich der Körper als fragmentierter unterschiedlichen Rollenbildern, in denen er jedoch nie aufgeht.

In den Arbeiten von Pola Sieverding werden Geschlechternormen immer wieder gebrochen, gleichzeitig jedoch Geschlechterklischees als wirkmächtig und performativ scheinbar bestätigt. Sie polarisieren die Gefühle des Betrachters beziehungsweise der Betrachterin jeweils

of their bodies. This effect is intensified by seeing the protagonists in extreme close-ups, individual body parts in motion, fragmenting the body and presenting its materializations as a search for different identities.

Queering Expectations

Pola Sieverding's prior works contained queer body enactments that negotiate gender norms and body images. Here we see something else, a queering of our expectations as observers, an undermining of certain normative ideas. It makes an absolute difference whether a man, a woman or another gender is observing these body images and what that spectator finds, or wishes to find, in them. Conventional definitions like "gender trouble" and "queer performance" do not seem to fit, since Pola Sieverding's prior works already even called into question new gender categories. An earlier work, *Make Up* (2010, ill. p. 7), shows the slow transformation of the masculine into the feminine. The scene: a makeup table at which a man becomes a diva through a slow process of transformation. The face is shown in close-up, the camera capturing the gaze in the intimate perspective of the mirror. The transformation tips, however, as lipstick is applied to make the mouth bigger and bigger, till at last the whole face glows signal red. The removal of the makeup, the deconstruction, is celebrated with the same slowness as the process of creation.

In another work, *Cross Metropolis Machine* (2012, ill. p. 8), which was shown in the Museum Abteiberg installation together with the wrestlers and boxers, we see a single female dancer at a club. The delicate movements of her fingers and arms at first seem to affirm a familiar image of dance as the movement of beautiful form. Yet she ceaselessly seeks new positions. Her gaze is directed straight into the camera, but seems trance-like, lost in herself. Zooming in on individual body parts that take on the appearance of detached living matter in the alternation of darkness and colored light, we approach the body as fragmented, as trying out different roles that never succeed.

Although gender norms are broken over and over again in Pola Sieverding's works, gender clichés appear as potent and performatively affirmed. Each work polarizes the viewer's feelings in a different way. This is because the photographs of the wrestlers and boxers do not in any way seem like medially normalized expressions

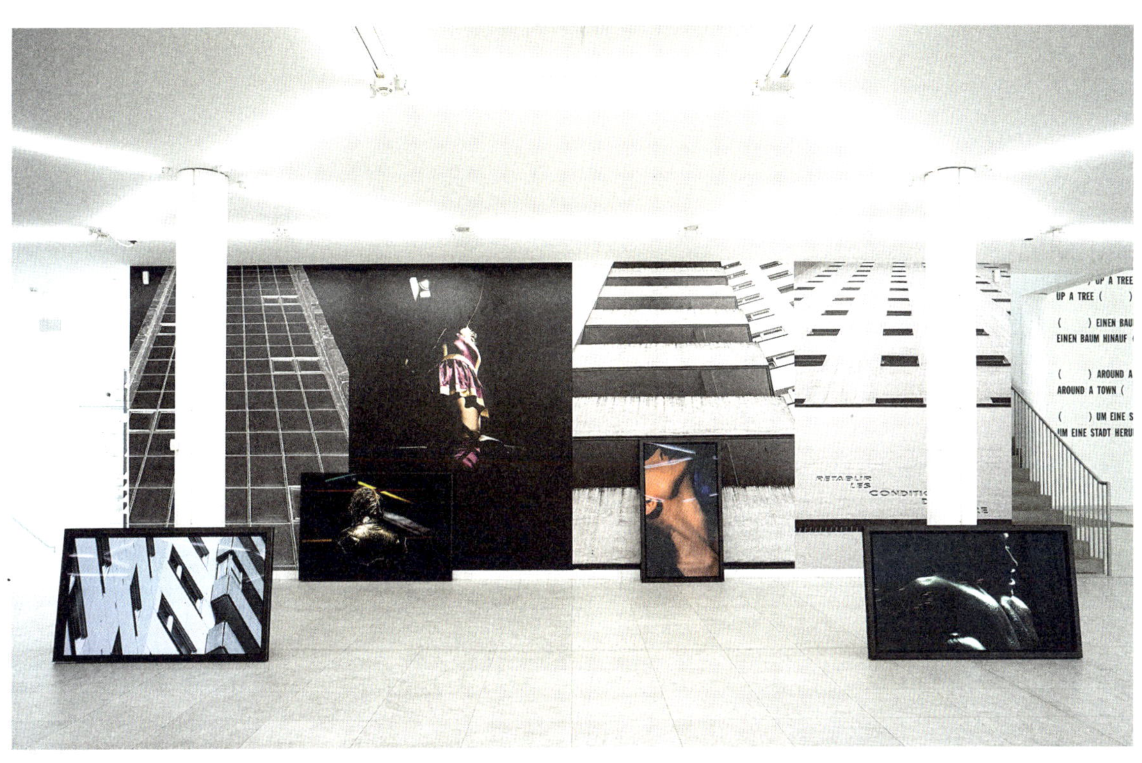
UP A TREE (   )
EINEN BAUM HINAUF
AROUND A TOWN (

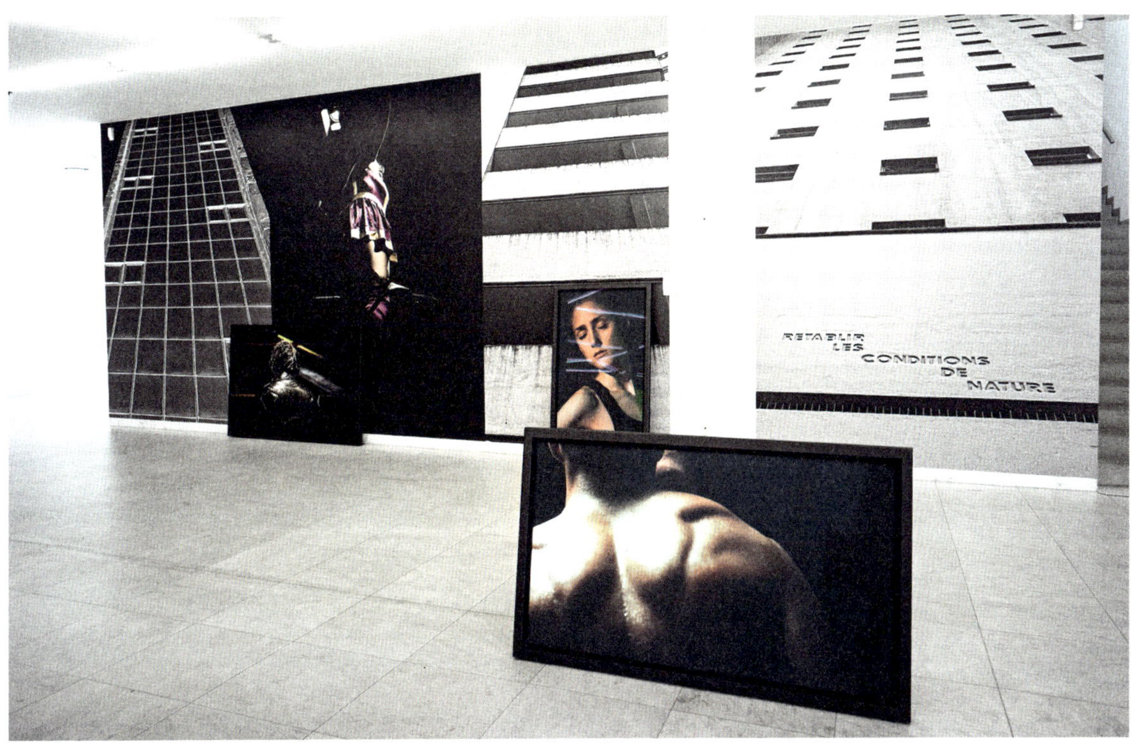
RETABLIR
LES
CONDITIONS
DE
NATURE

unterschiedlich. Denn keineswegs erscheinen die Fotografien der Wrestler und Boxer als medial normalisierter Ausdruck einer massenkulturellen Überblendung von Körper und Bild. Auch die Posen und Gesten sind wie bei der Tänzerin in Sieverdings Videoarbeit *Cross Metropolis Machine* nicht etwa durchdrungen von einer simplen Kritik des Bildes in den Massenmedien. Sie arbeiten vielmehr daran, den jeweiligen Einsatz des eigenen Körpers als Bild seiner Transparenz und Offensichtlichkeit zu befreien. Als »Tanz« verschiedener Bewegungsformen, als Choreografie des Raumes und der Konstellationen in ihm, als Inszenierung von Körperbildern stellt Pola Sieverding die Performanz von Geschlecht, von Selbst- und Fremdbild im Zuge einer feministischen Aneignung explizit aus.

Die performativen Körper, die in jenen Schemata schon aufgrund der panoramatischen Anordnung nicht aufgehen, erinnern in ihrer Ambivalenz vielmehr daran, dass der sowohl in kulturkritischen als auch in affirmativen Theorien gezogene Kurzschluss, der visuelle Kultur und Konsum in eins blendet, hier nicht aufgeht. Das Sehen-Fühlen wird einer konsumistischen Ökonomie nicht entgegengesetzt, sondern zeigt gerade ihre Verwobenheit.

Materiale Affizierung mit Hindernissen

Trotz der verschiedenen Ebenen der Inszenierung wird der offensive Blick in die Kamera bei den Wrestlern und Boxern stets vermieden, es ist nicht der Moment der konfrontativen, herausfordernden Pose, des Spektakels – die Aufnahmen vermeiden den expliziten Blickkontakt mit dem Kameraauge, wie er in der Fotografietheorie so oft als entscheidend hervorgehoben wurde. Vielmehr scheint die Kamera direkt zwischen die Kämpfenden zu fahren. Doch geht es hier auch nicht um einen dokumentarischen Charakter. Was also bewirkt die empfundene Nähe, auf welcher Ebene entsteht sie?

Die Pose – zwischen Tableaux und Szene, zwischen zwei Bewegungen – konstituiert eine Momentaufnahme, zwischen Fotografie und Choreografie der Bewegung und ihrer Installation im Raum bringt sie etwas auf den Punkt, das mich als Betrachterin berührt. Diese Affizierung bringt mich selbst in den Zustand des *in-between*, als schlüpfte ich in die Rolle des Mediums; es situiert die Empfindungen nicht lediglich in meinem Blick, sondern mein Körper vermittelt jene Repertoires des Affekts. Etwas zeigt sich, etwas kommt zur Erscheinung zwischen Bild und Bewegung, und es ist dieses

of a mass cultural merging of body and image. Likewise, the poses and gestures, as with the dancer in Sieverding's video *Cross Metropolis Machine,* are not permeated, for example, by a simple critique of the image in mass media. The poses and gestures endeavor instead to free each deployment of one's own body as an image of its transparency and obviousness. Pola Sieverding explicitly exhibits the performance of gender, of the image of the self and the other, in the course of a feminist appropriation, as a "dance" of different forms of movement, as a choreography of space and configurations in space, as the mise-en-scène of body images.

The performative bodies that do not fit into that scheme, not least because of their panoramic arrangement, are instead a reminder in their ambivalence that the shortcut pursued in cultural criticism and affirmative theories alike, that of conflating visual culture and consumption, does not work here. Seeing-feeling is not opposed to, but rather interwoven with a consumerist economy.

Materializing Affect and Intrinsic Obstacles

Despite the different levels of staging, the wrestlers and boxers never gaze aggressively into the camera. What we see here is not the moment of the confrontational, provocative pose, of the spectacle. The images avoid explicit visual contact with the camera's eye, a contact so often emphasized as decisive in photography theory. Instead the camera seems to move directly between the fighters. Yet this work also does not seek a documentary character. What, then, is effected by the experience of closeness, on what level does it arise?

The pose—between tableaux and scene, between two movements—constitutes a snapshot. Between photography and choreography of movement and its installation in space, this snapshot gets to the heart of something that touches me as an observer. This power of affect brings me into the state of being the "in-between," as though I were slipping into the role of the medium. Sensations are situated not solely in my gaze; rather my body transmits those repertoires of affect. Something shows itself, something becomes visible between image and movement, and it is this moment of what is potential that charges the range of poses so strongly with affect.

The theatricality and the dramatics inherent to the images not only tie them into a progression of before and after but create an "afterlife of images" in Aby Warburg's

Moment des Potenziellen, das die Register der Posen so affektiv auflädt.

Die Theatralität und Dramatik, die den Bildern eignen, spannen sie nicht allein in einen Verlauf des Davor und Danach, sie schaffen ein »Nachleben der Bilder« im Warburg'schen Sinne: In der Kombination der Bilder und ihrer Register verweisen dieselben auf zahlreiche andere und erstellen so ein Geflecht von Bezügen, die jedoch keinesfalls allein auf der Ebene operieren, auf der Bilder Sinn erzeugen, sondern darüber hinausgehen und sich uns quasi als Empfindungen vermitteln.

Die Affinitäten und Konflikte zwischen Bildrepertoires sind letztlich auch Mittel der kinematografischen Montage, und es ist der Film, der wie keine andere Kunstform als *das* Medium der Affektionen, des Melodramas oder auch der immersiven Verstrickung gilt. Auf fotografischer Ebene ist die Situation, das Drama des Wrestling-Kampfes in den singulären Momenten eingefangen, in der Installation wiederum werden diese erneut verknüpft, und es scheint ein filmisch-theatrales Setting zu sein, das sie uns erfahren lässt.

Affekte, die durch den Körper hindurchgehen und ihn verändern, werden in den Körpern der Wrestler, der Boxer oder der erwähnten Tänzerin nicht nur sichtbar – sie verlassen die Ebene der reinen Sichtbarkeit und werden zwischen den Ebenen der Wahrnehmung als ein auch kinästhetisch, imaginativ und affektiv Verbundenes spürbar.

Das Wrestling als eine unwiederbringliche Verausgabung des Körpers erinnert ebenso wie der Tanz an die temporäre Verfasstheit unserer Körperlichkeit und daran, wie konstitutiv diese für unseren Weltbezug ist. Die Übertragung einer Empfindung konstituiert uns als unabgeschlossene Subjekte, die sich im Akt der Betrachtung zwischen Individuellem und Allgemeinem, zwischen affektivem Potenzial von Bildern und der Verortung innerhalb eines Markts von Bildern positionieren. Pola Sieverdings Arbeit reflektiert gekonnt den Prozess der Wiederaneignung von Affekten, die nicht die eigenen sind. Bewusst geht sie damit um, dass der symbolische Tauschwert im Rahmen einer Ökonomie der Affekte entscheidend ist. An dieser Ambivalenz setzt ihre Arbeit an.

sense: Through the combination of images and their ranges, the images refer to numerous other images and thus create a network of connections operating not only on the level on which images create meaning but beyond it, conveying themselves to us as a sort of sensation.

The affinities and conflicts between image repertoires are ultimately means of cinematographic montage as well. Film, more than any other art form, is regarded as *the* medium of affect, melodrama and immersive involvement. On the photographic level, the situation, the drama of the wrestling match is captured in singular moments. In the installation, by contrast, these are linked anew to one another, and there appears a filmic and theatrical setting that lets us experience these moments.

Emotions that go through the body and change it are not only rendered visible in the bodies of the wrestlers, the boxers or the dancer we have mentioned, but depart from the level of pure visibility and become tangible between levels of perception as something that is also kinesthetically, imaginatively and affectively linked.

Wrestling as an irretrievable exertion of the body recalls, like dance, the temporary constitution of our corporeality and how constitutive this is for our connection to the world. The transmission of a sensation constitutes us as subjects who are not self-contained, positioning ourselves in the act of observation between the individual and the general, between the affective potential of images and within a market of images. Pola Sieverding's work skillfully reflects on the process of reappropriating affect that is not one's own. She is deliberate in her approach to the fact that symbolic exchange value is decisive in an economy of affect. This ambivalence forms the springboard for her work.

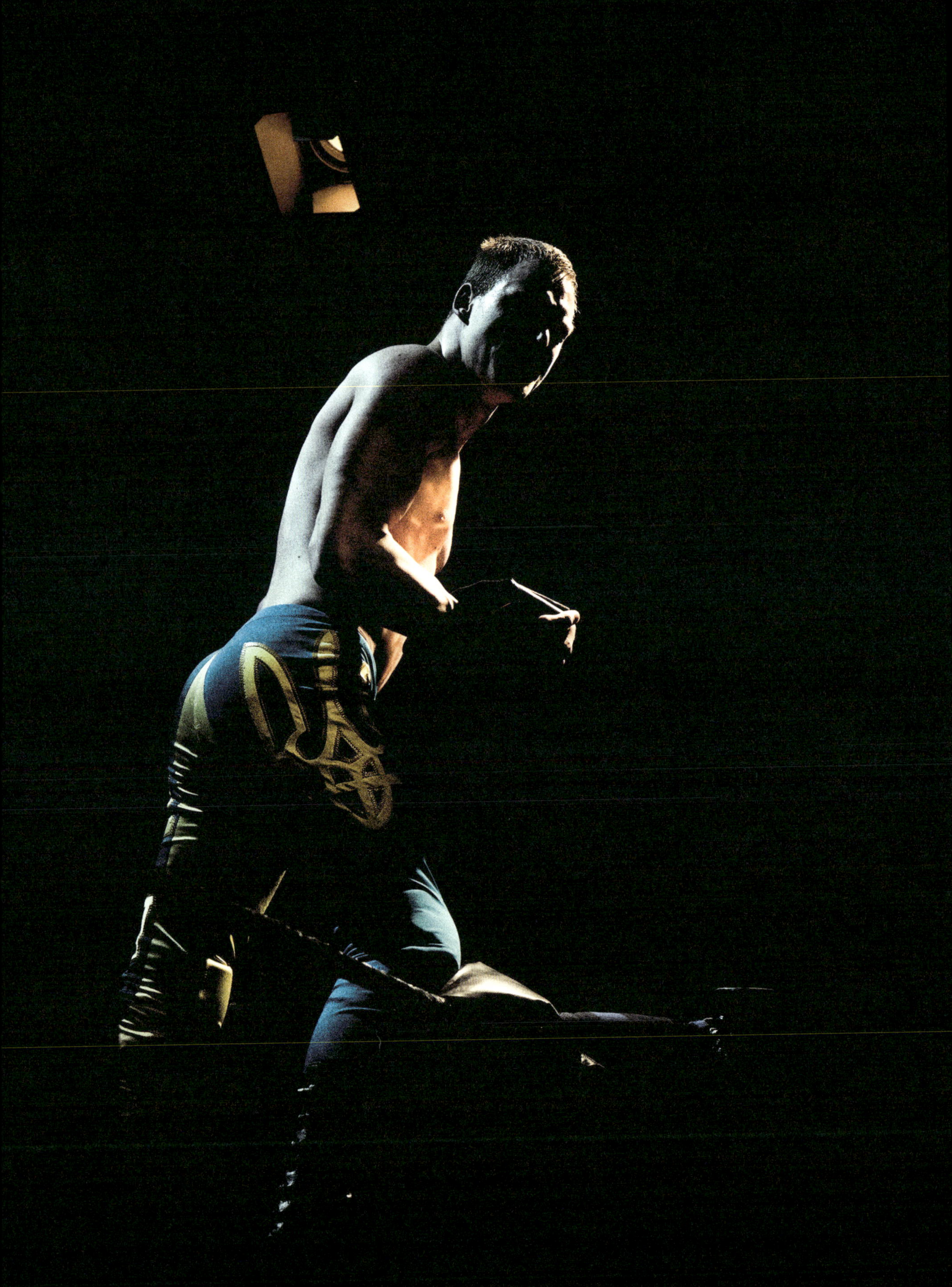

THE EPIC

NAK NEUER AACHENER KUNSTVEREIN

AUSSTELLUNGSANSICHTEN / INSTALLATION VIEWS
THE EPIC

2016
NAK Neuer Aachener Kunstverein

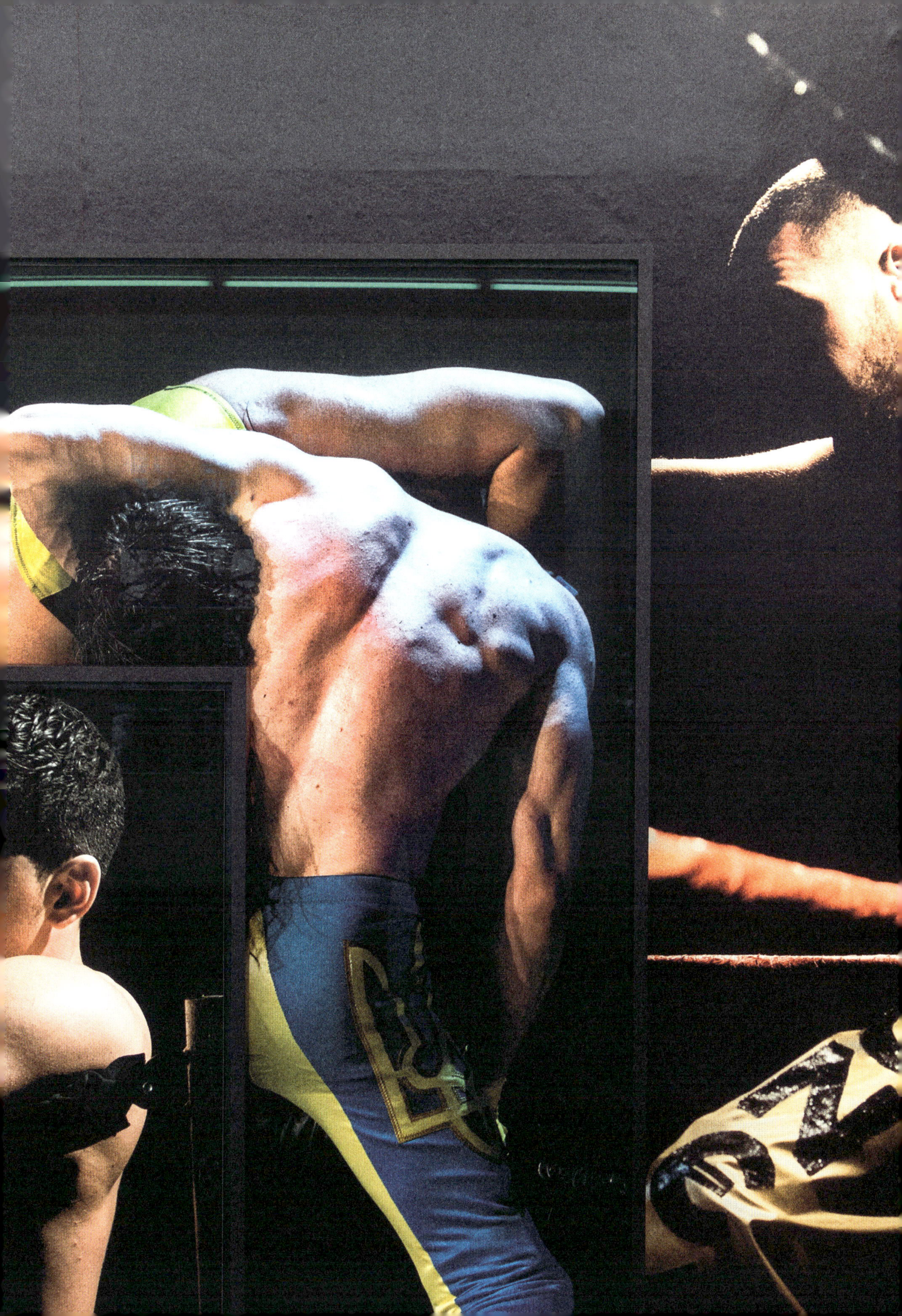

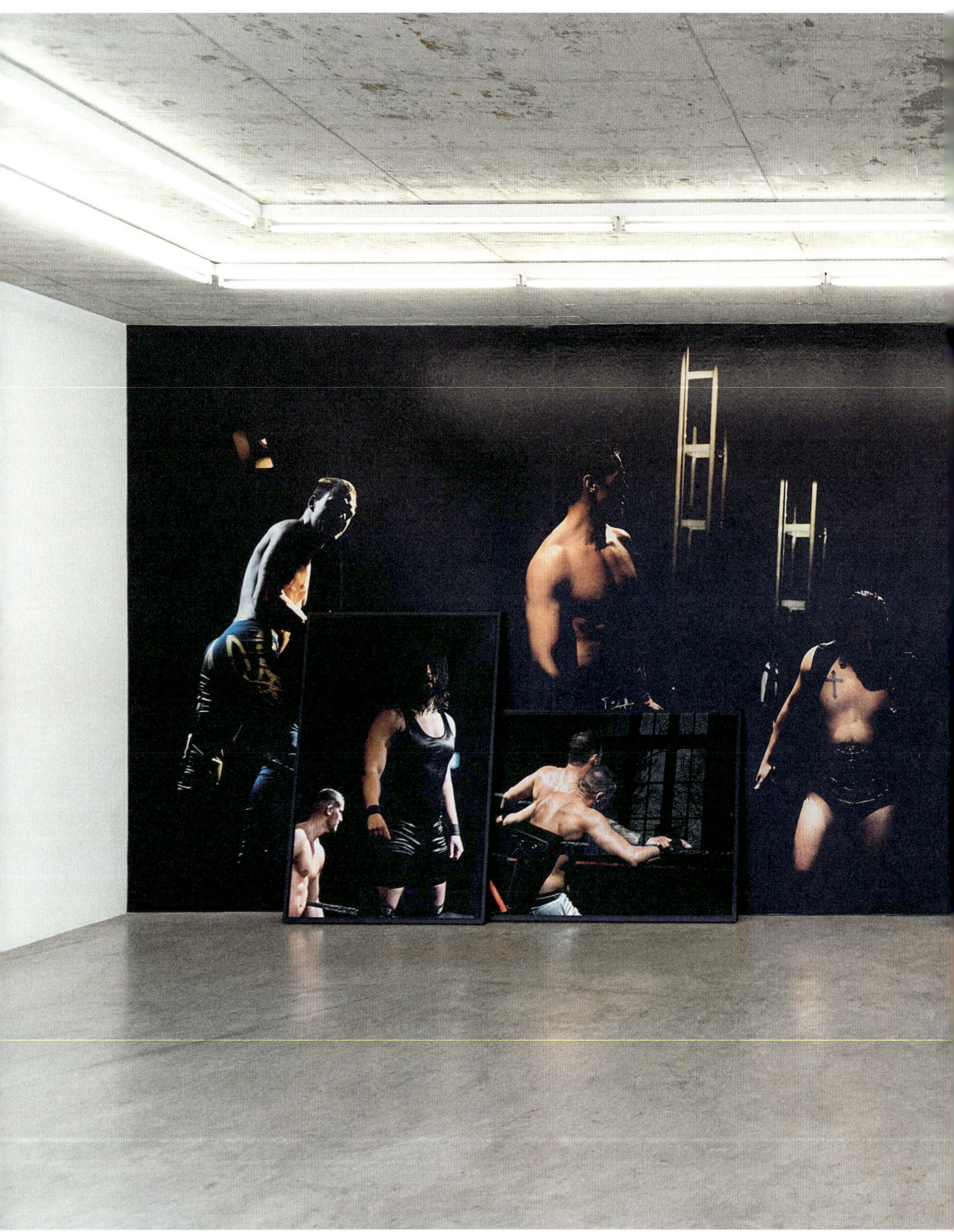

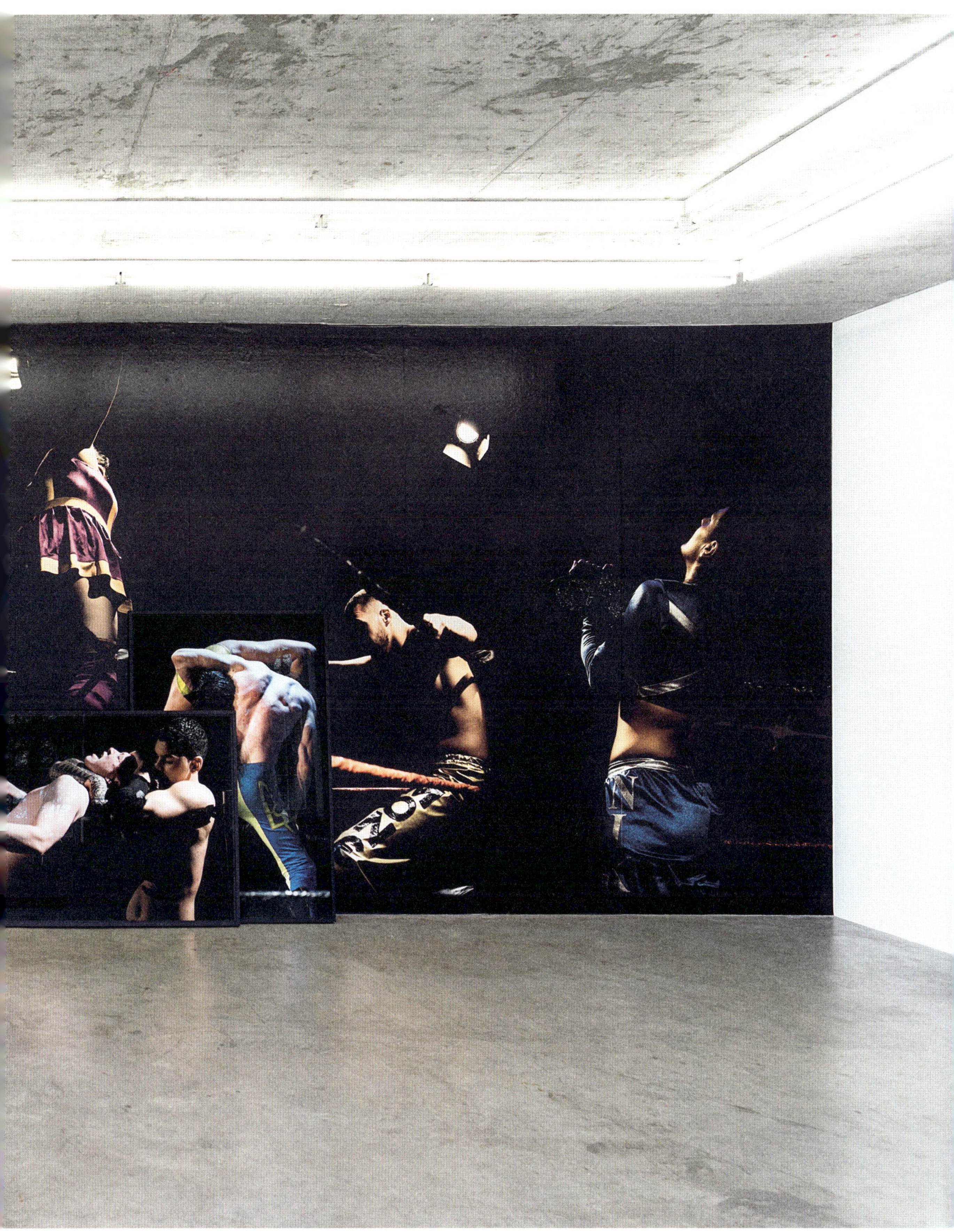

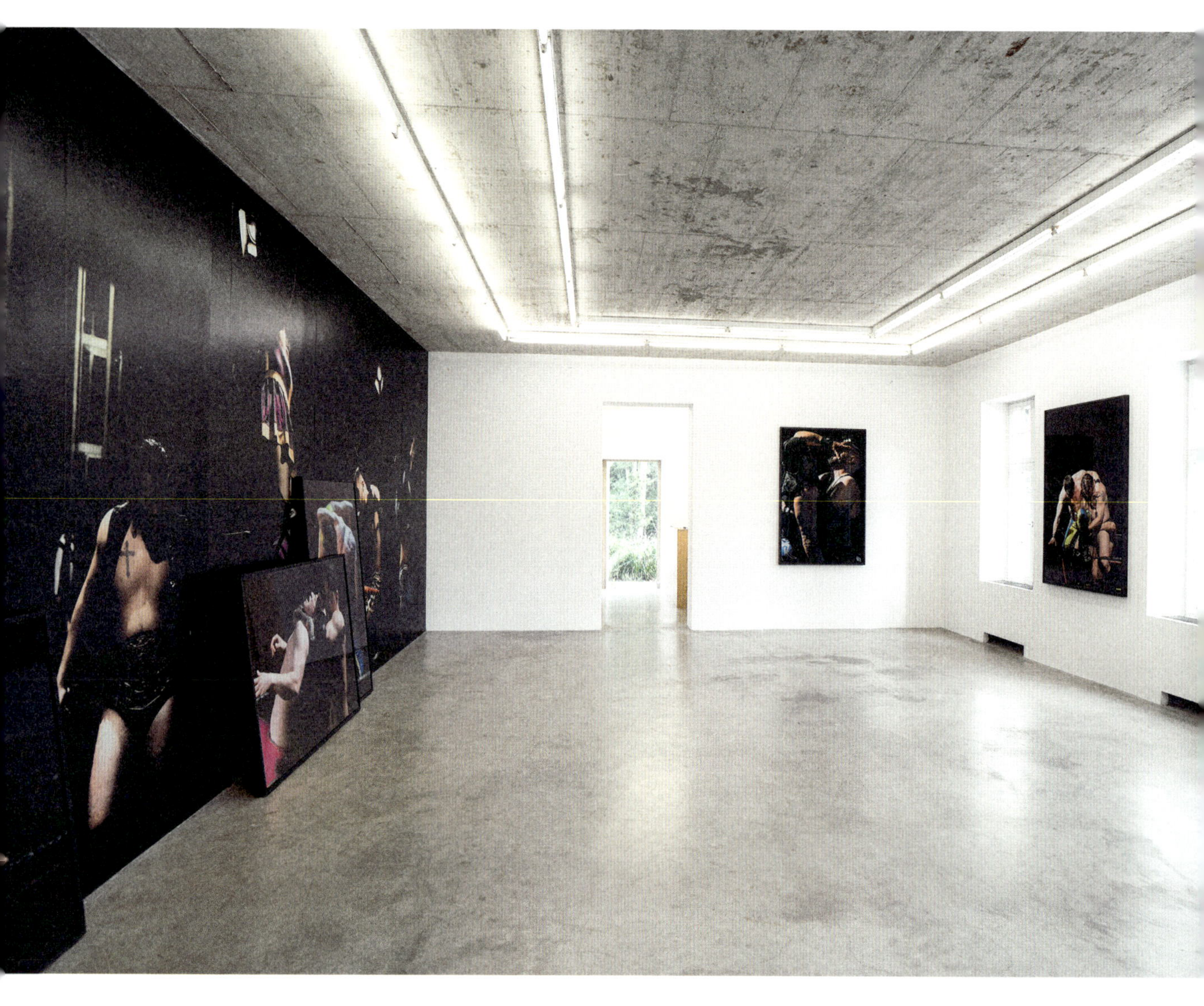

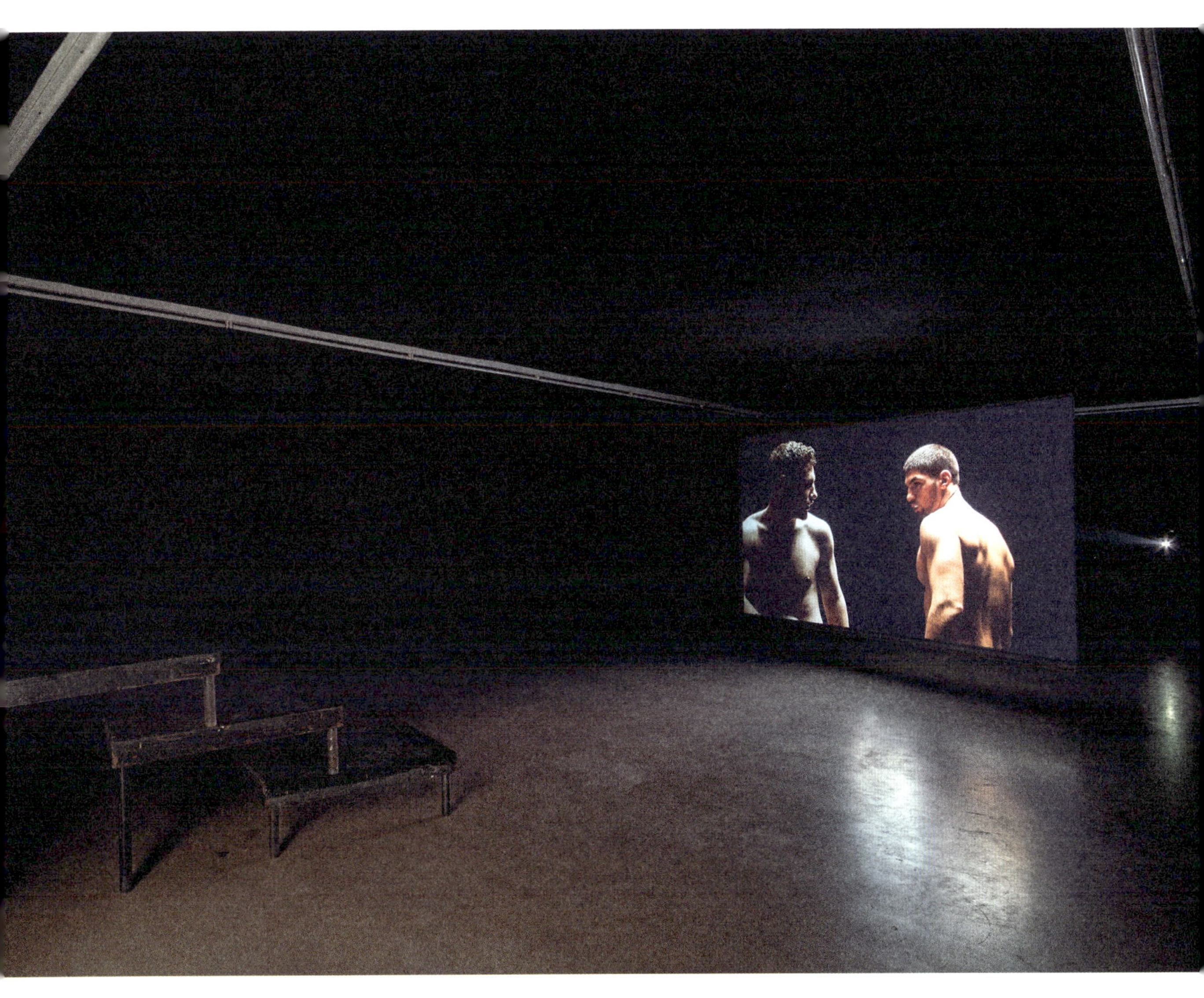

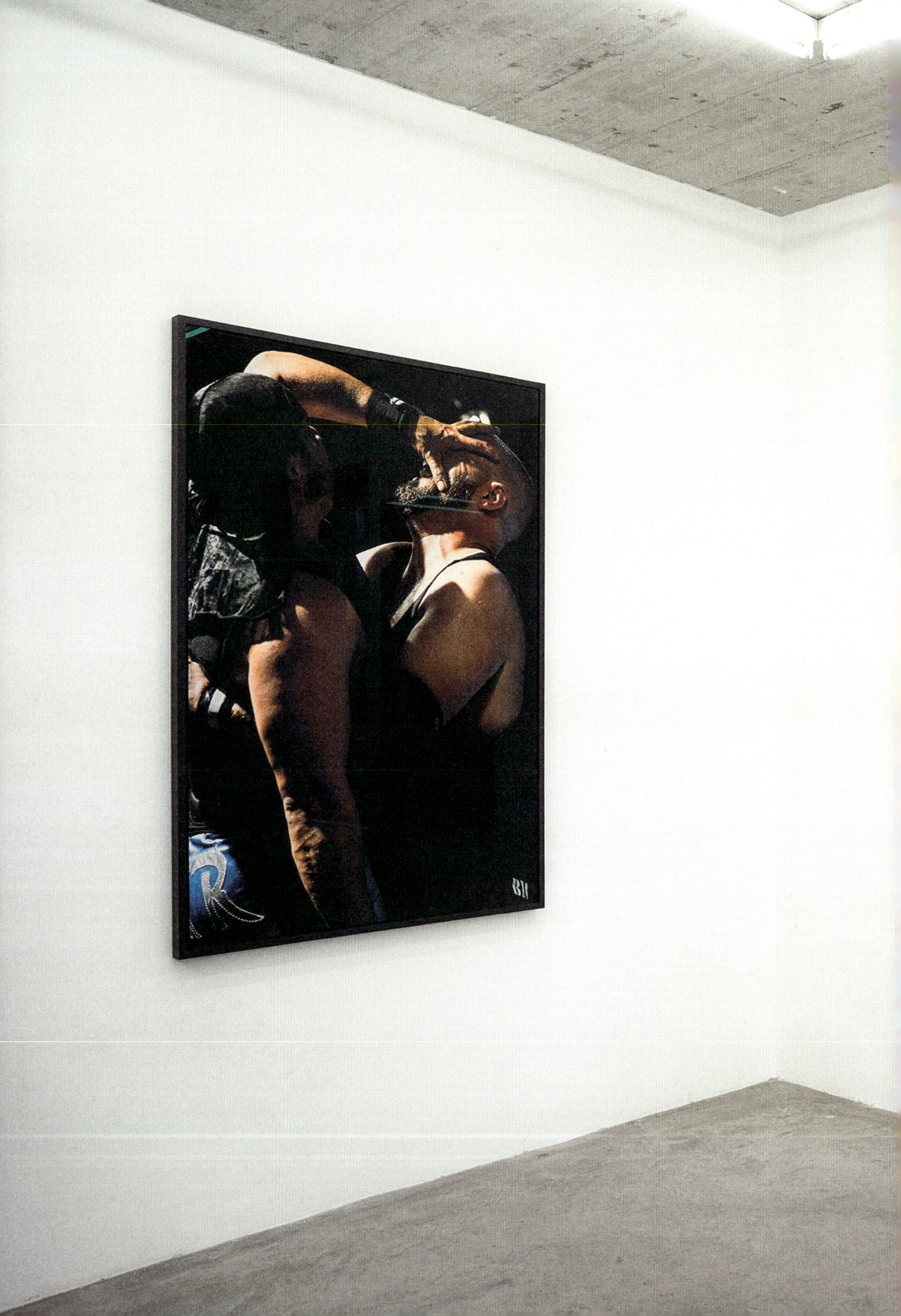

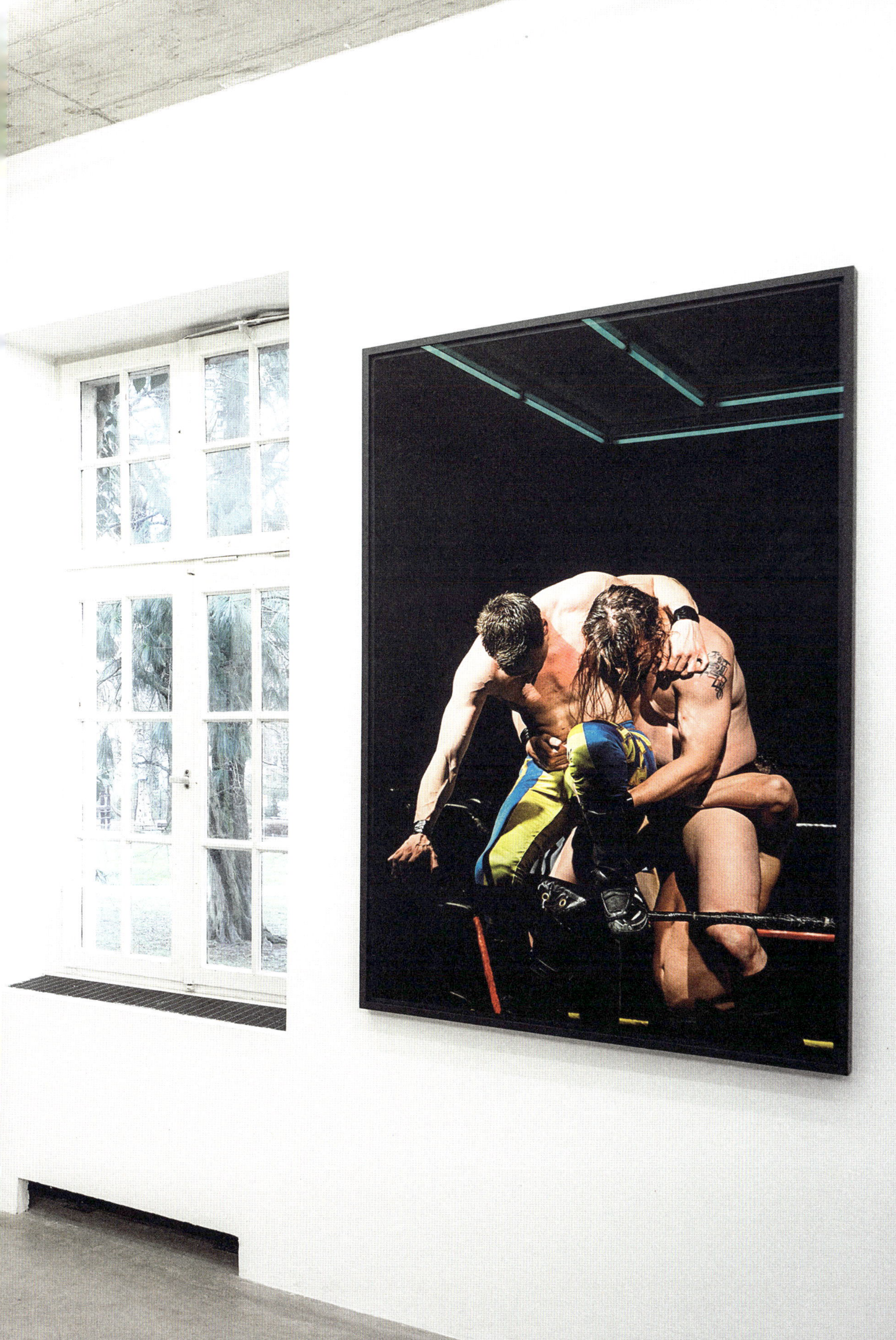

SLAM DOWN.
ÜBER DIE ZERSCHLAGUNG
DER INSZENIERTEN POSE
BEN KAUFMANN

SLAM DOWN:
ON SMASHING THE ENACTED POSE
BEN KAUFMANN

Protagonisten, mindestens zwei oder mehrere, die sich mit- und gegeneinander positionieren, sich verbal attackieren. Mit übertriebenem Gestus türmen sie sich auf, stürzen hinab oder schlagen zu, um den Kontrahenten akrobatisch auf Bretter, Boden oder Seile zu schicken und im Angesicht des Triumphes gründlich zu demütigen. Es sind Rollenspiele einer archaischen Männlichkeit innerhalb von Geschlechterrollen. Die Wrestlerinnen stehen den männlichen Kollegen in nichts nach. Die Adaption von evolutionsbiologisch dem männlichen Geschlecht zugeschriebenen Attributen wie Demonstration von Stärke, Alphatiergehabe oder auch Verherrlichung von Gewalt könnte positiv als Emanzipation interpretiert werden, letztlich bestätigt diese Nachahmung die patriarchalischen Züge des Wrestlings jedoch noch zusätzlich. Ad absurdum führte der US-amerikanische Entertainer Andy Kaufman die geschlechtliche Rollenverteilung und Zuordnung bereits Anfang der 1980er-Jahre, indem er im Wrestling ausschließlich gegen Frauen antrat.

Das Spektrum der Wrestling-Klischees, das als Rattenschwanz mit auf die Bühne geschleift wird, ist groß, und diese Vor- und Unterstellungen befeuern das Spektakel immer wieder aufs Neue.

Im Kontext des Wrestlings über die strategische Verwendung von Posen zu sprechen ist interessant, weil sich die Pose an sich über ihre Omnipräsenz in den sozialen Medien schon lange von ihrer ursprünglichen Intention einer exklusiv bildhaften oder skulpturalen Unmittelbarkeit verabschiedet hat. Trotz allem bedingen sich Pose und Inszenierung noch immer gegenseitig. Für diese Abhängigkeit kann die Pose reichlich wenig. Auch wenn sie hätte aufbegehren oder sich zumindest wehren können im Sinne von »Stop – nicht mit mir!«. Es scheint fast so, als hätte sich die Pose mit der Zeit selbst potenziert und folglich entkörpert, um sich dem mobilen Bildschirm gegenüber zu behaupten. Inhaltlich resultiert dies in einer kurzen Halbwertszeit, denn gerade durch die Nachahmung beziehungsweise ihre mediale Distribution und ständige Verfügbarkeit hat die Pose entschieden an Bedeutung verloren. Jene beeindruckende wie publikumswirksame, für den einen Moment gültige Pose wirkt durch unzählige Wiederholungen beliebig und blass. Als scheinbar letzter Ausweg bleibt ihr, gemäß dem Motto »Ich mach jetzt mal einen auf 3D-Druck« zur Plastik zu erstarren und zu hoffen, damit den »Lucky Punch« gesetzt zu haben.

Protagonists, at least two, sometimes more, positioning themselves with and against each other, attacking each other verbally. With exaggerated gestures, they climb up, jump down and strike back, acrobatically bringing their adversary to the boards, the floor or the ropes in a deeply humiliating act just seconds away from victory. This is the role-playing of an archaic masculinity. These female wrestlers are in no way inferior to their male colleagues. The adaptation by women of things attributed to male biological evolution, including demonstrations of strength, alpha-animal airs and the glorification of violence, could be interpreted positively as emancipation. Yet in the end, this imitation only reaffirms wrestling's patriarchal qualities. After all, the American entertainer Andy Kaufman was already taking the assignment and attribution of gender roles to the absurd in the early 1980s, when he competed as a wrestler who only fought women.

The innumerable wrestling clichés are dragged onstage too, a kind of baggage, and these ideas and innuendos drive the spectacle forward again and again.

It is interesting to consider the strategic use of poses in the context of wrestling because the pose in itself, through its omnipresence on social media, long ago departed from its original intention of exclusively visual or sculptural directness. All the same, pose and enactment continue to be dependent on one another. The pose can do very little to change this dependency, even if it could rise up or at least defend itself and shout: "Stop, count me out!" The pose almost seems to have multiplied and thus disembodied itself over time, just so it could assert itself on the displays of our smartphones. In content, the consequence is a short half-life, because imitation, or rather the distribution and continual availability of imitations through digital media, has caused the pose to diminish considerably in significance. Every pose that is impressive, that reaches audiences and has validity for a moment is made interchangeable and fades through countless repetition. The apparent last resort of the pose is to solidify into plastic and leap on the bandwagon of the 3D print, in the hope that by doing so it will land that illusive "lucky punch."

How do pose and enactment coexist in the photographic works of Pola Sieverding? The concentration is on the fighters, female and male. They seem to have been cut out with a scalpel, standing in the spotlight in front of an emptied, infinitely black backdrop. The protagonists function in and of themselves, as though acting from an

Wie koexistieren Pose und Inszenierung in den fotografischen Arbeiten von Pola Sieverding? Die Konzentration liegt auf den Kämpfer/-innen, die in den fotografischen Arbeiten scheinbar mit dem Skalpell freigestellt wurden und im Rampenlicht vor entleerter, unendlich schwarzer Kulisse stehen. Die Protagonisten funktionieren aus sich selbst heraus, wie aus einer intrinsischen Motivation. Der klischeebeladene und im Kollektivgedächtnis verankerte Plot des Wrestlings ist nach innen gewendet – stumm, schwarz und im kognitiven Sinn mächtig. Das umgebende Schwarz weist Bezüge zum Science-Fiction-Film auf, wenn die Kamera lautlos durch das All schwebt, wenn Zeit und Ort vermeintlich ausgehebelt sind und die Devise lautet: »Alles schon vorbei oder wieder möglich«.

Im Kontext der Ausstellung werden die Arbeiten noch entschieden intensiviert, indem sich überlebensgroße Wrestler/-innen in Form von gerahmten Fotoarbeiten dezidiert über die komplette Ausstellungswand und davor skulptural verteilen. Pola Sieverding nutzt jene zu Anfang beschriebene Inszenierung zwischen einem Minimum an Dokumentation und einem Maximum an Pathos oder, um in der Bildsprache zu bleiben, sie reduziert den Ton- und Informationswert auf das Notwendigste und konnotiert dies mit dem jeweils individuellen Dasein des Rezipienten. Wrestling und Existenz verschmelzen. Es handelt sich nicht mehr um eine collagenartige Szenerie einzelner Posen, es sind einfach Bilder, es sind Substrate.

Die inszenierte Pose wird zerschlagen, sie wird defragmentiert und eröffnet so die Loslösung von besagten Klischees hin zu einem diskursiven Raum, einem Raum der Verhandlung.

intrinsic motivation. The plot of wrestling, laden with clichés and anchored in collective memory, is turned in upon itself: silent, black and powerful in the cognitive sense. The surrounding black calls to mind a science-fiction film in which the camera silently floats through outer space, when time and place seem abolished and the rule of the day is something like: "Everything's over, or possible all over again."

In the exhibition context, the works are decisively intensified further through the larger-than-life-size wrestlers being emphatically and sculpturally placed, as framed photo works, across and in front of the entire exhibition wall. Pola Sieverding's style of theatrical staging employs a minimum of documentation and a maximum of pathos. In visual terms, she reduces the sound and visual details to the bare necessities and connotes them on the basis of each individual viewer's own being. Wrestling and existence melt into one another. This is no longer a collage-like scenery of individual poses. These are simply images. These are substrates.

The enacted pose is smashed, defragmented. The release of the pose from clichés opens up into a discursive space, a space of negotiation.

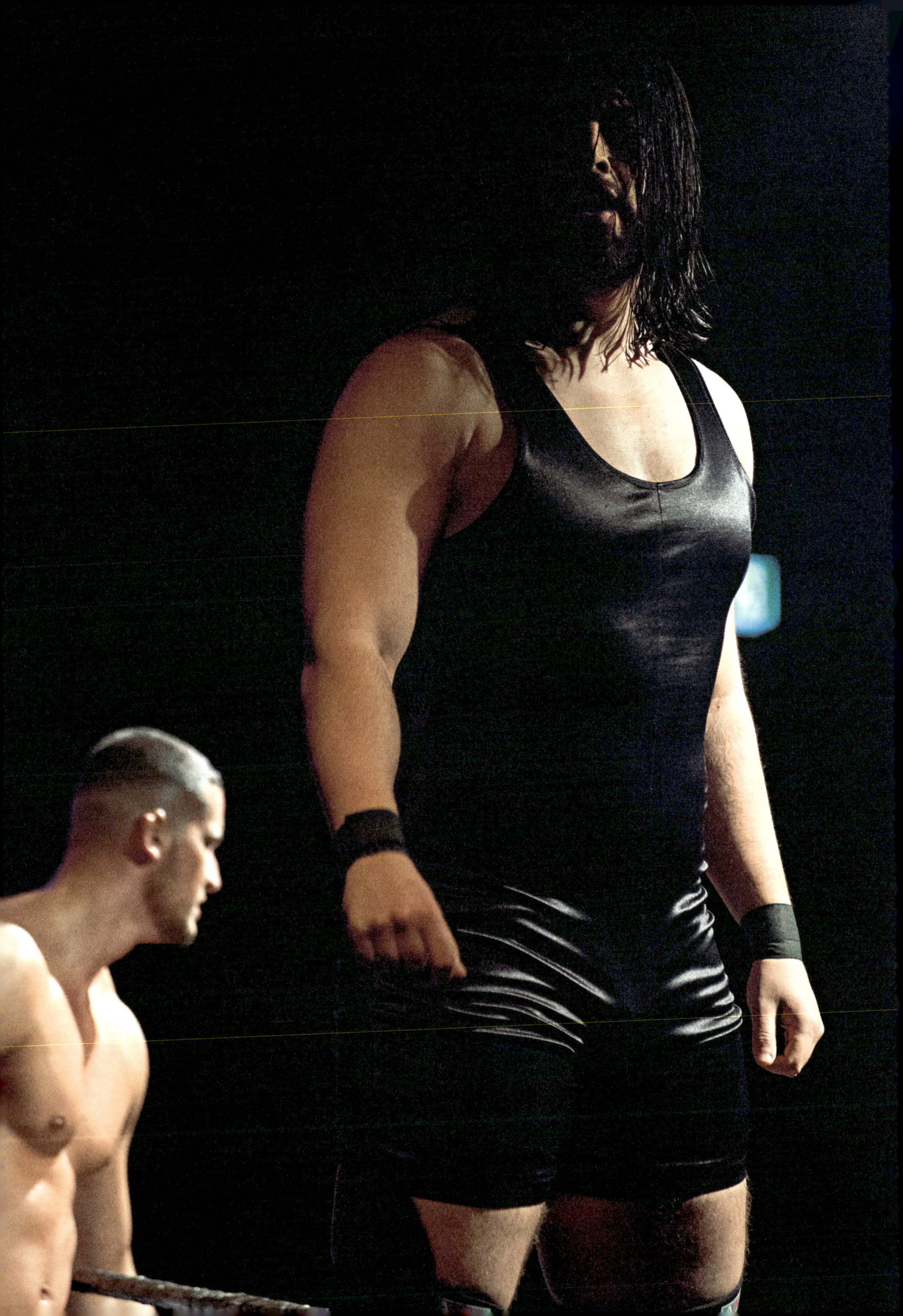

ARENA

ARENA
#2, #5, #7, #3, #12, #11, #10, #6, #9, #8, #1

2014
Pigmentdruck auf Papier / Pigment print on paper
167,8 × 111,8 cm
111,8 × 167,8 cm

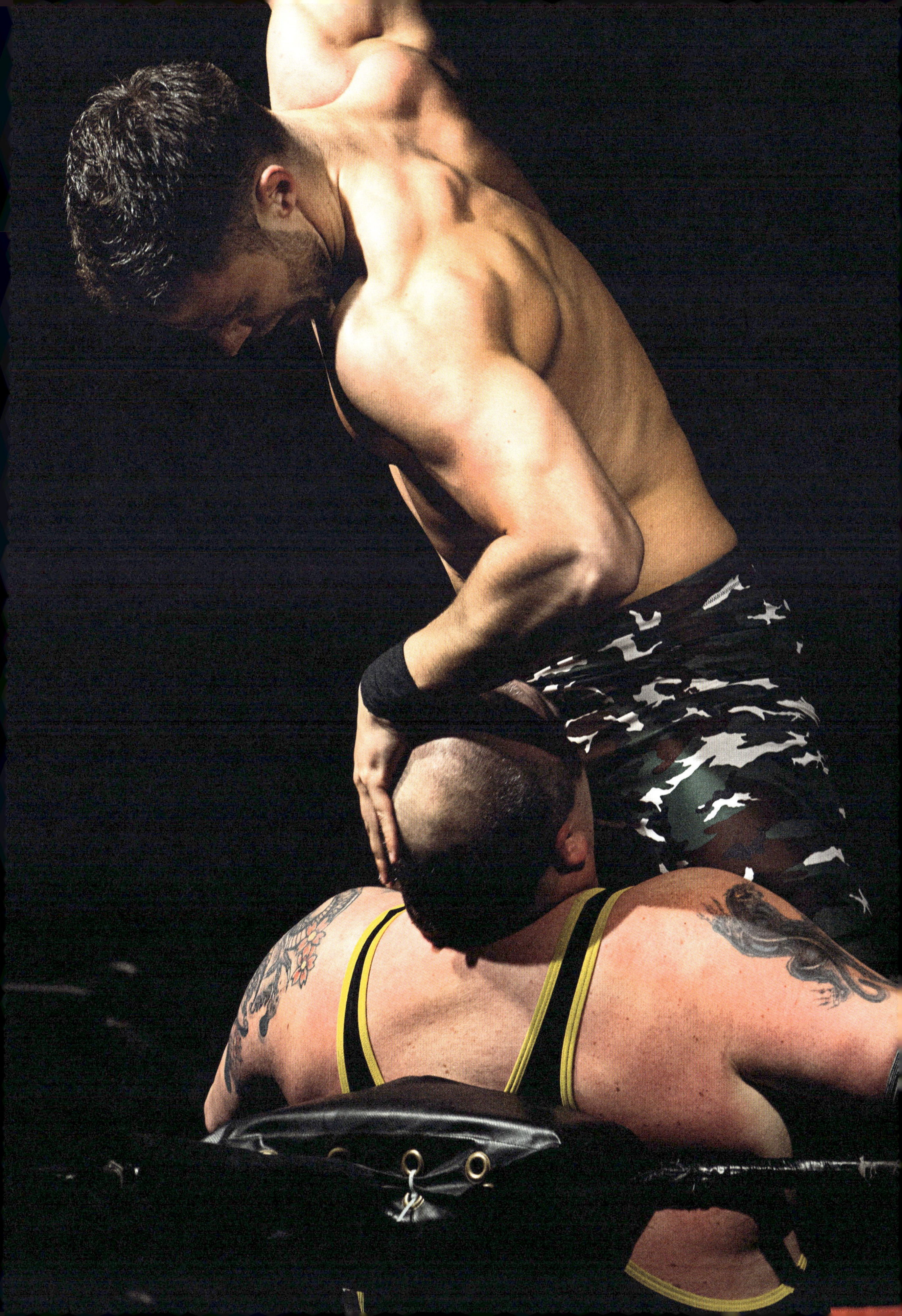

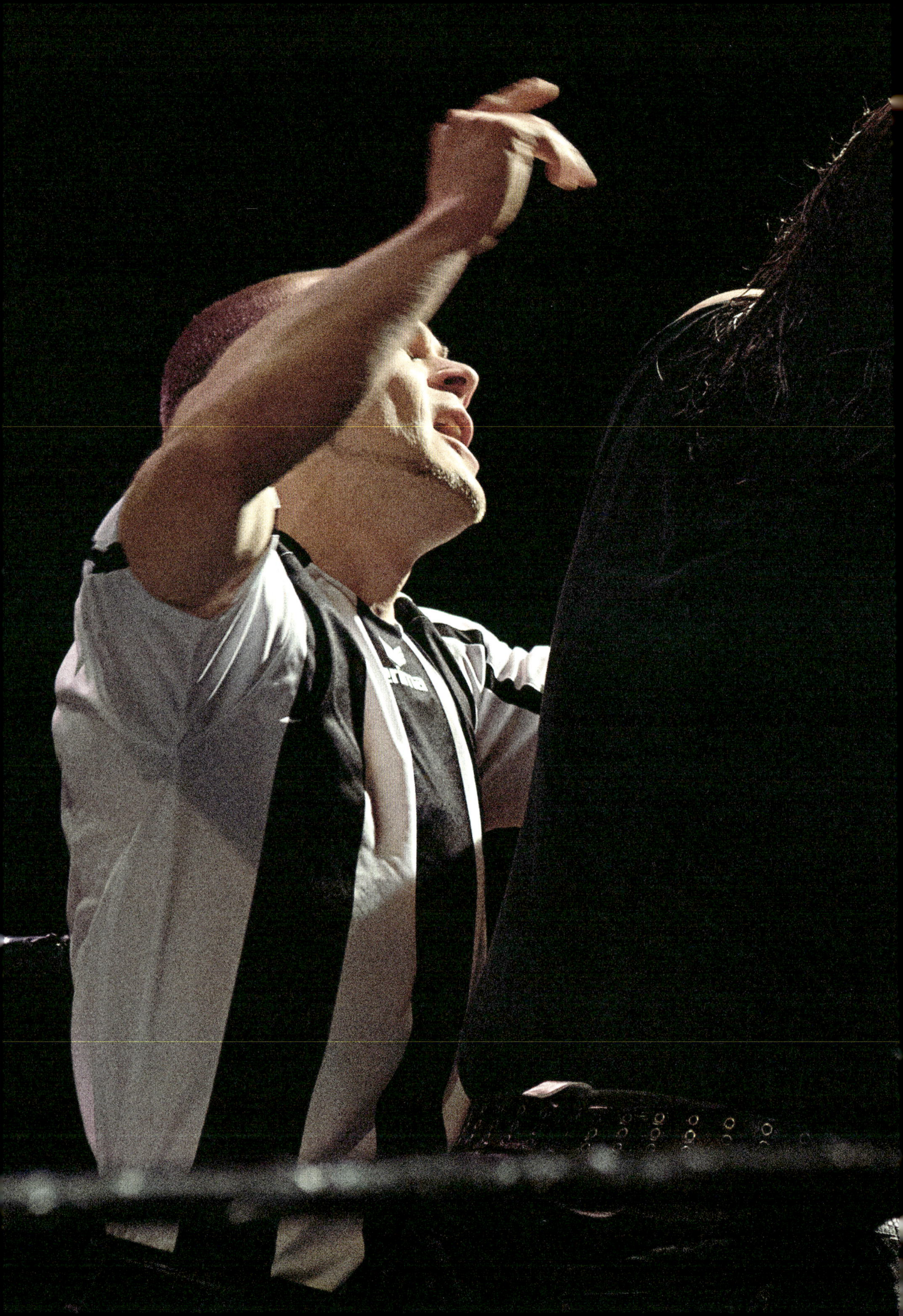

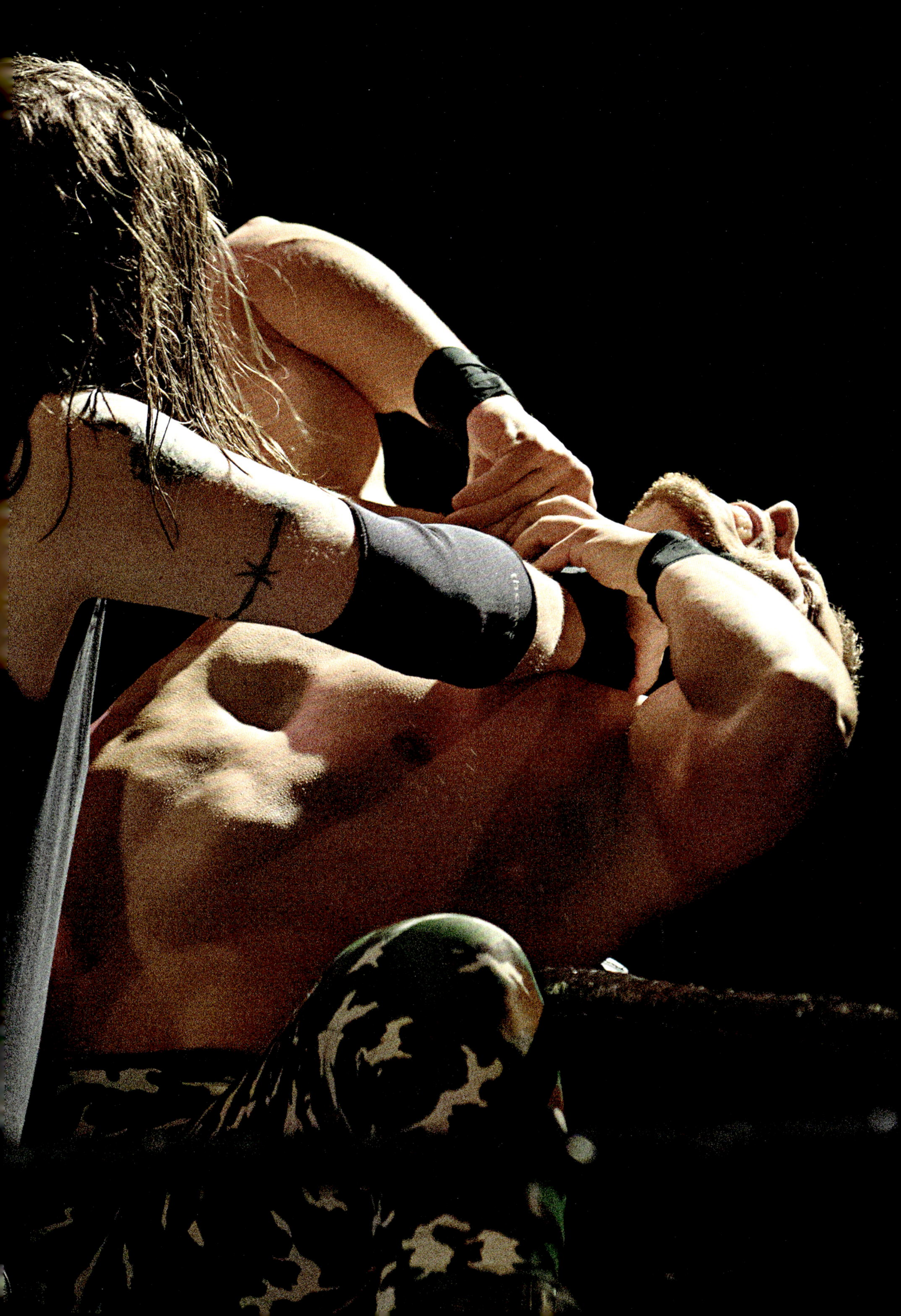

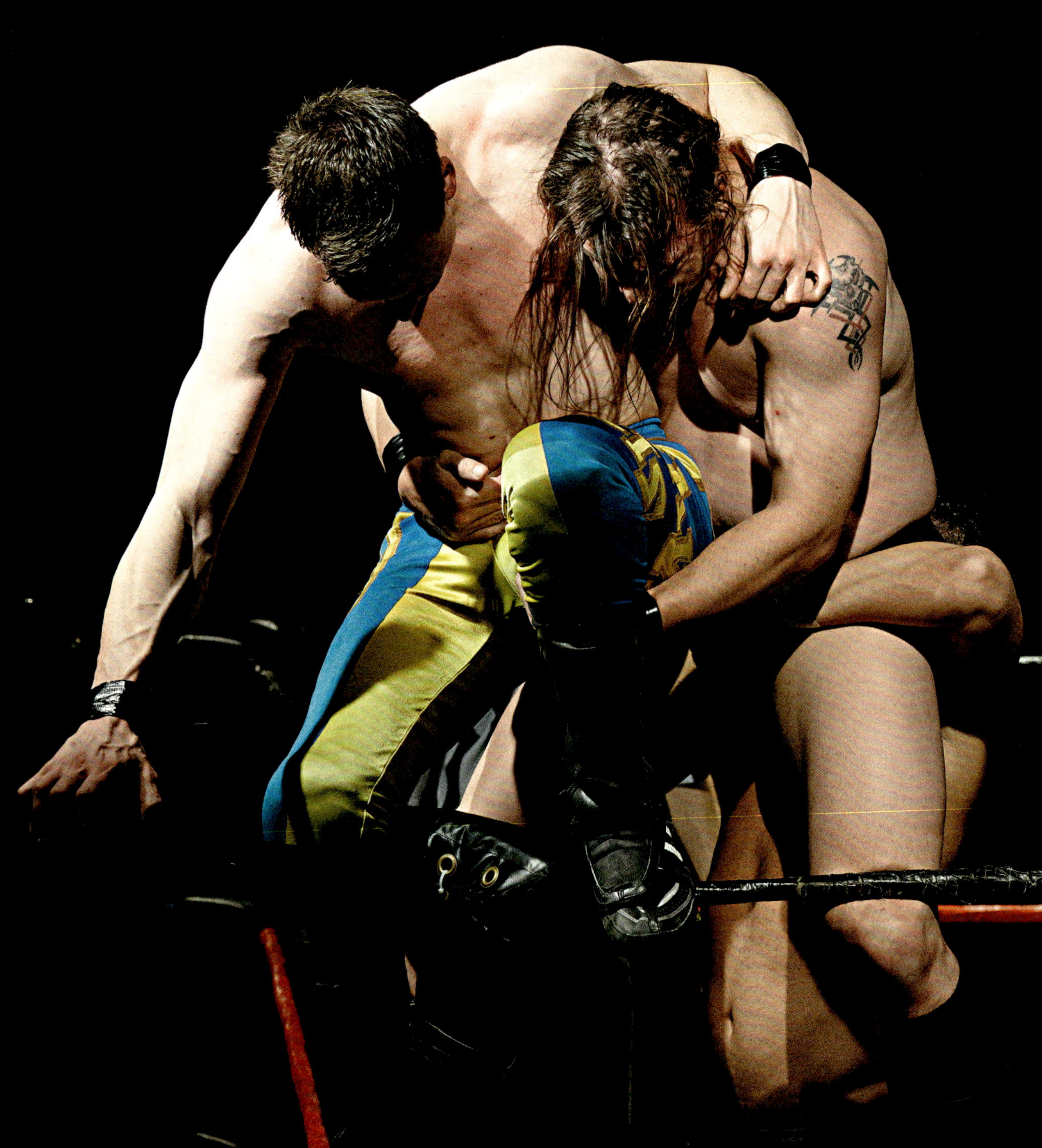

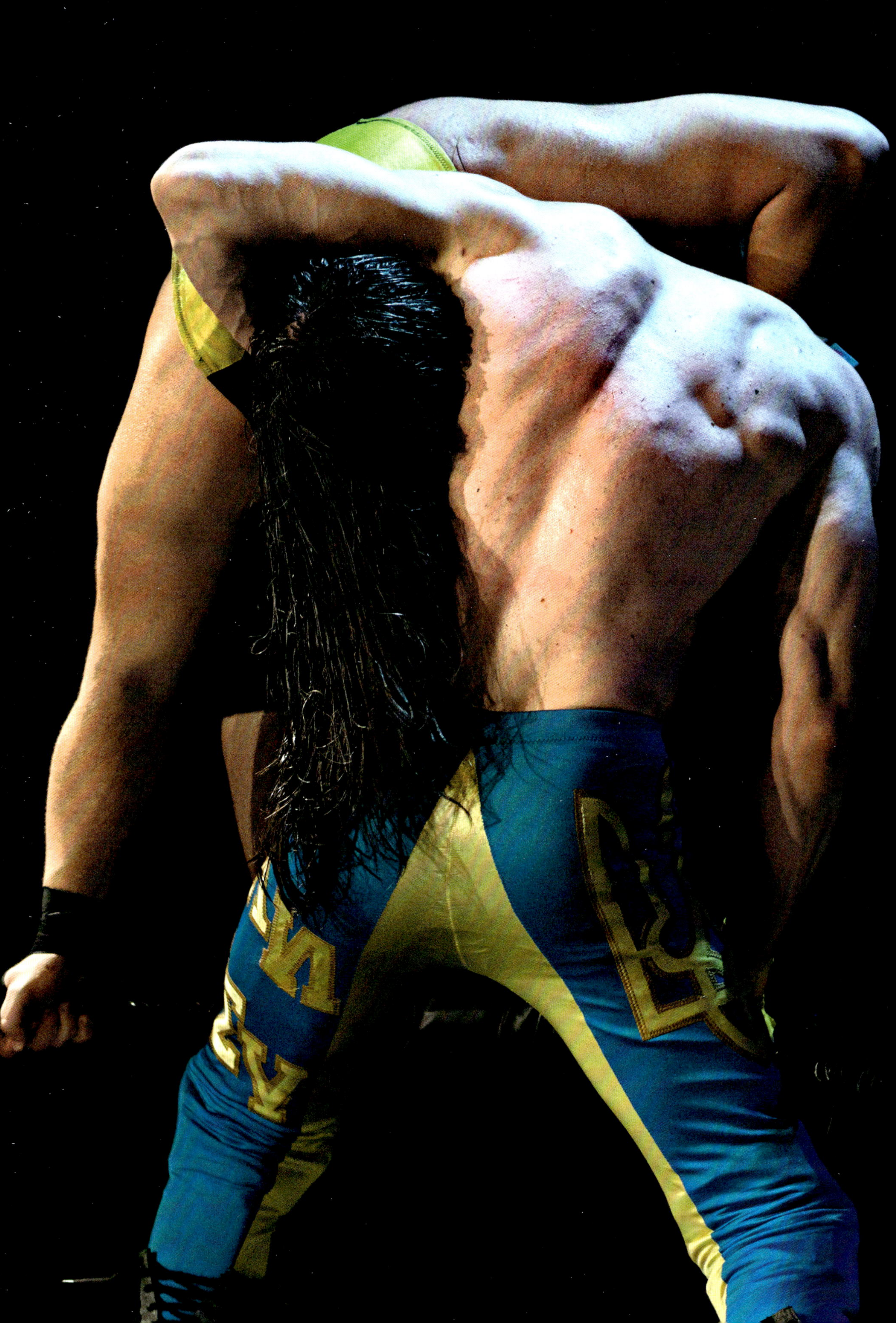

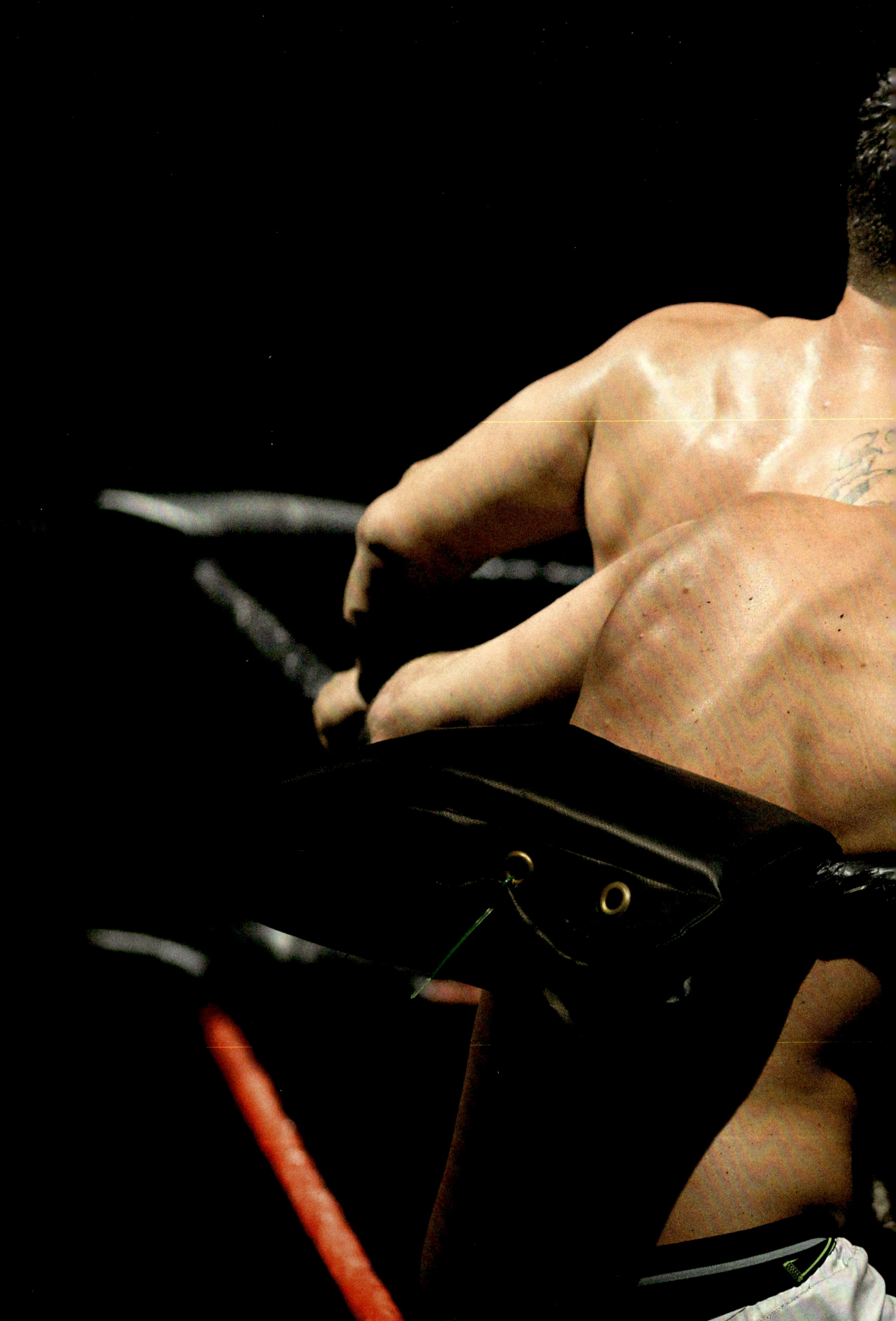

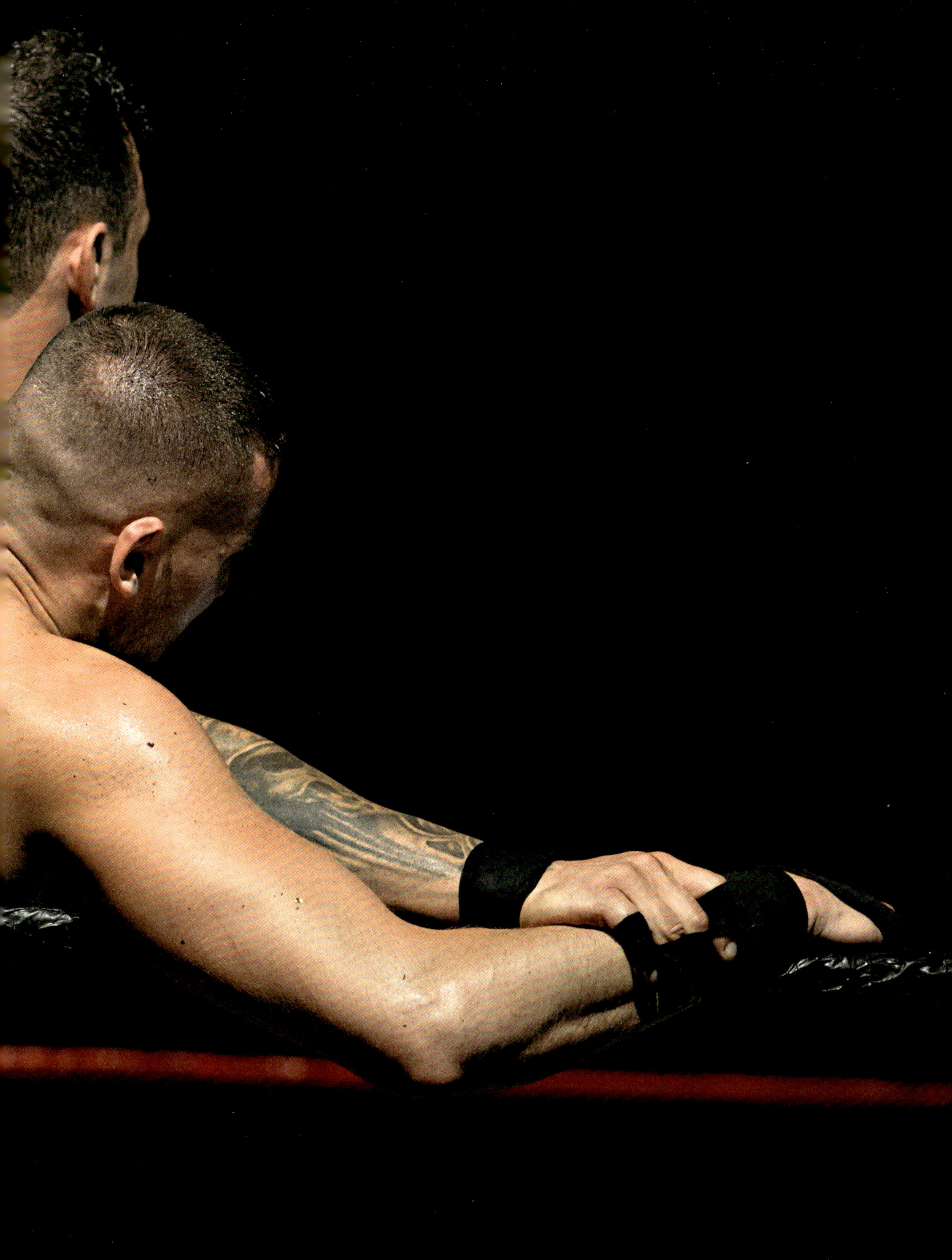

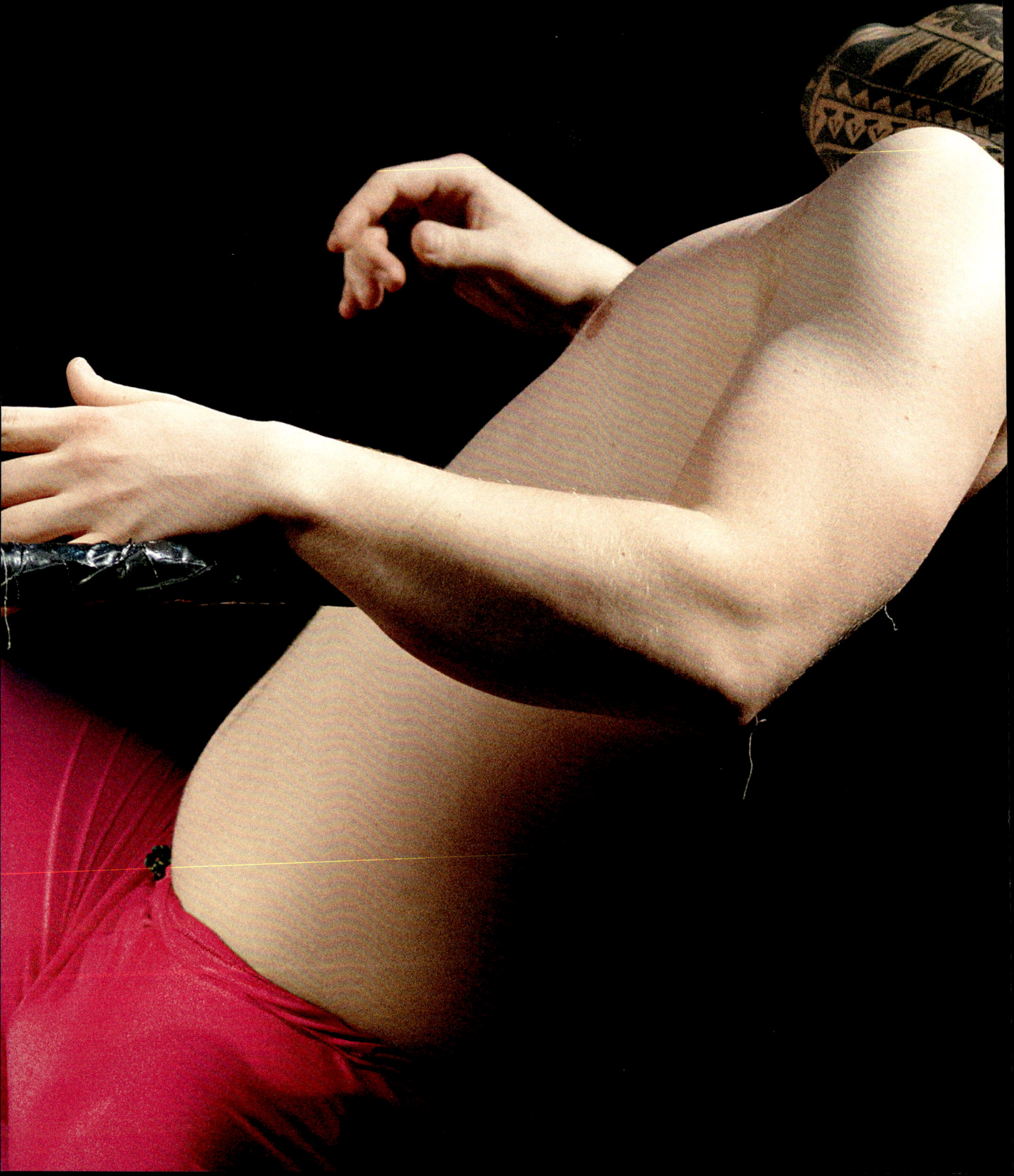

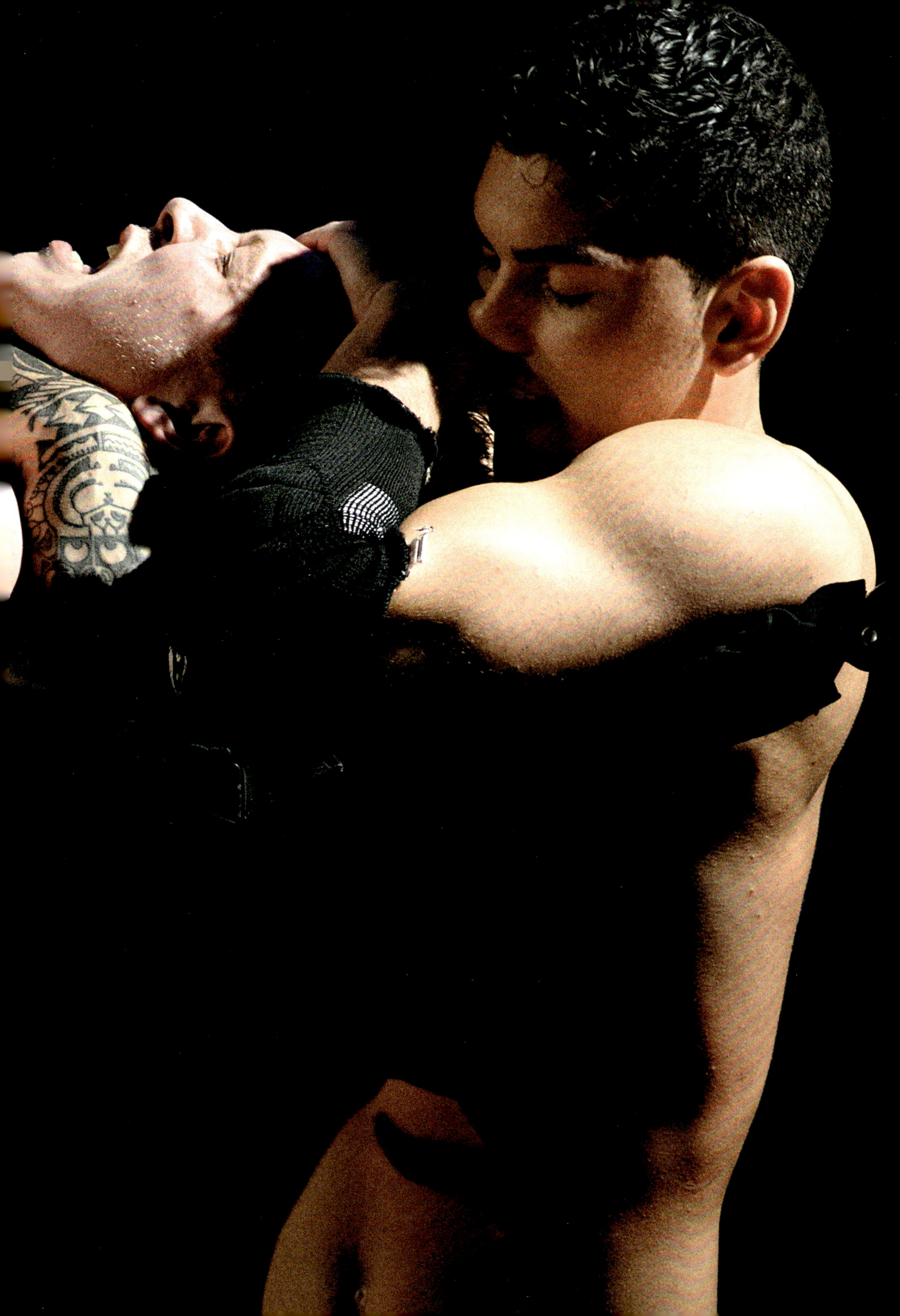

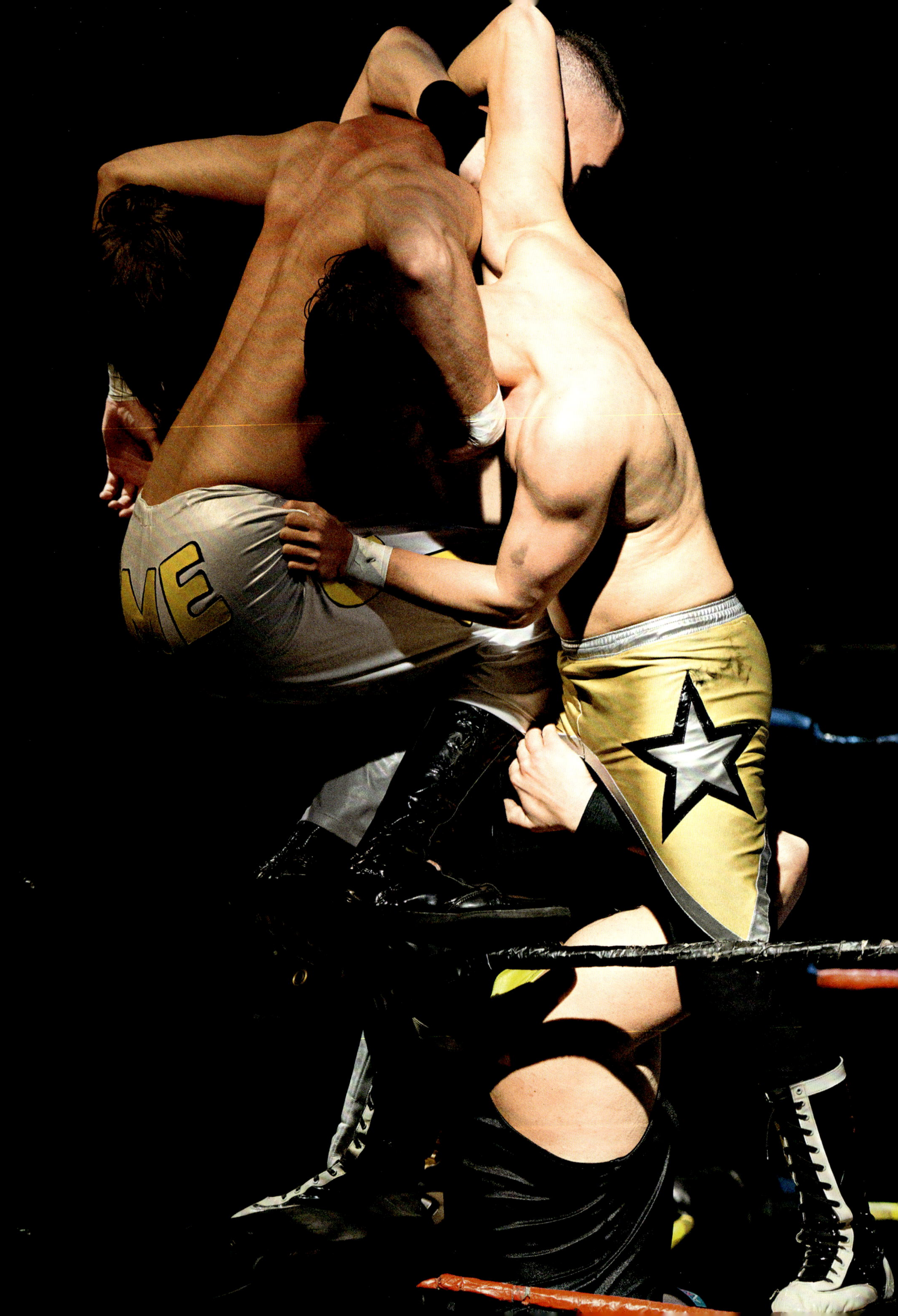

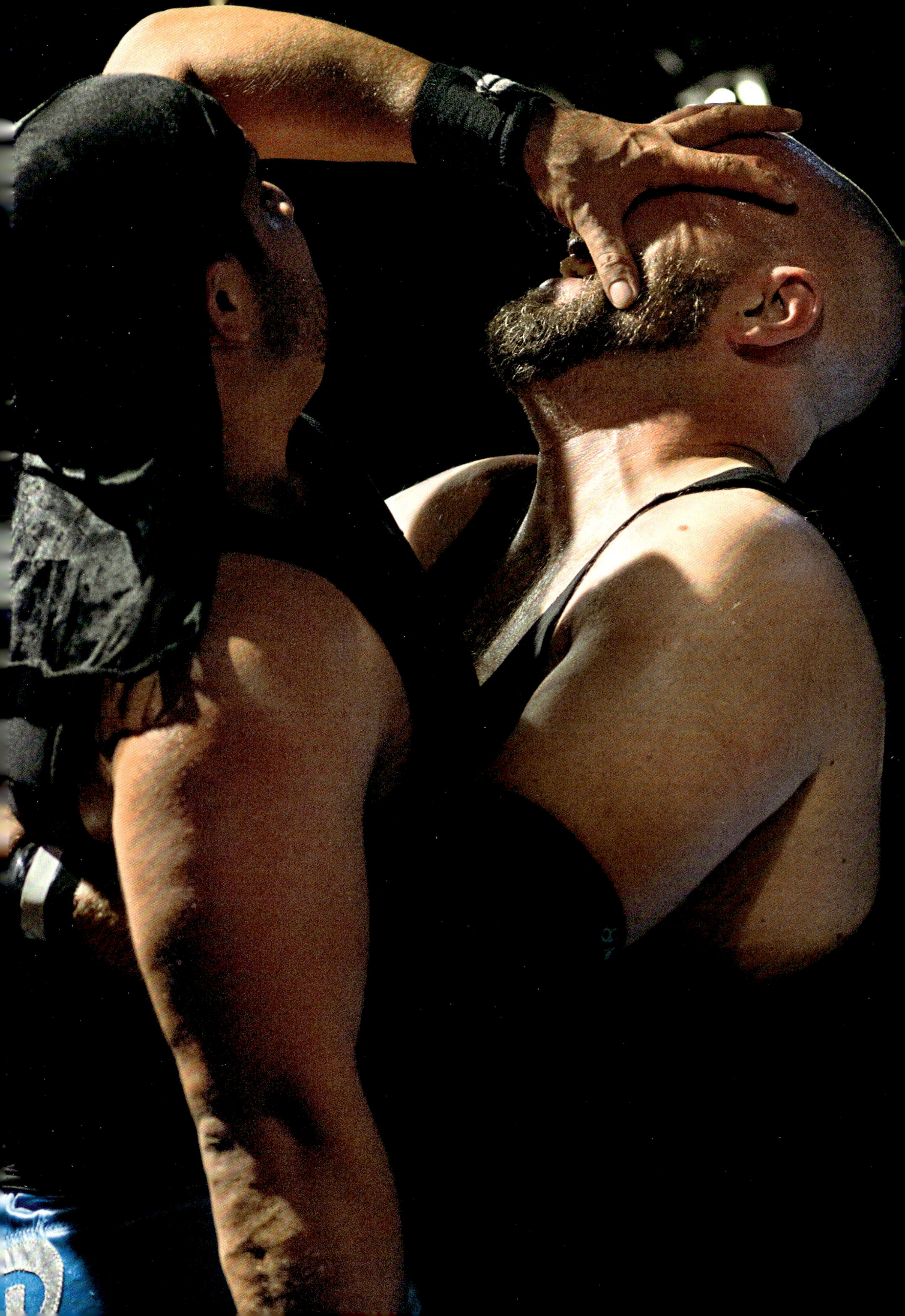

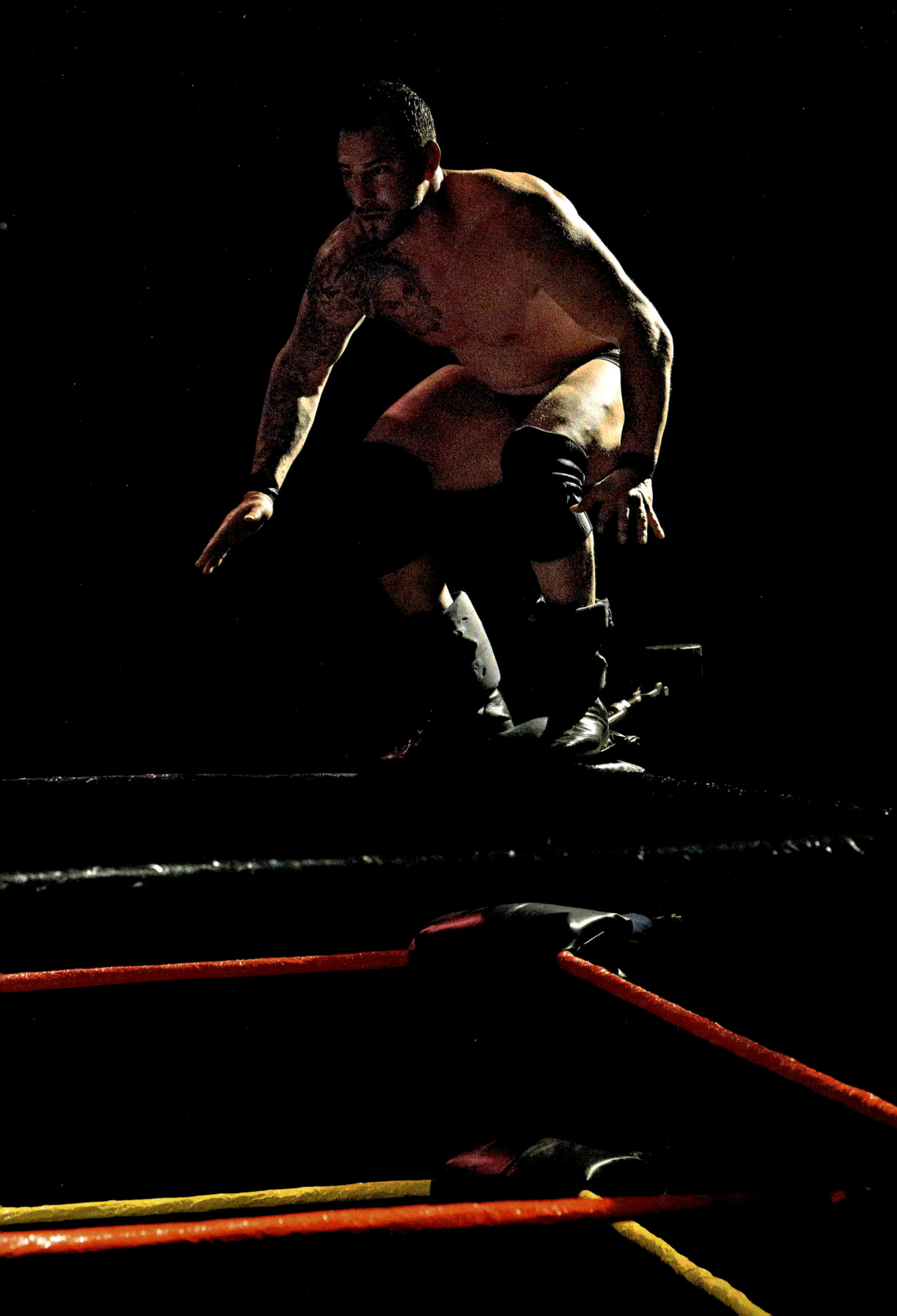

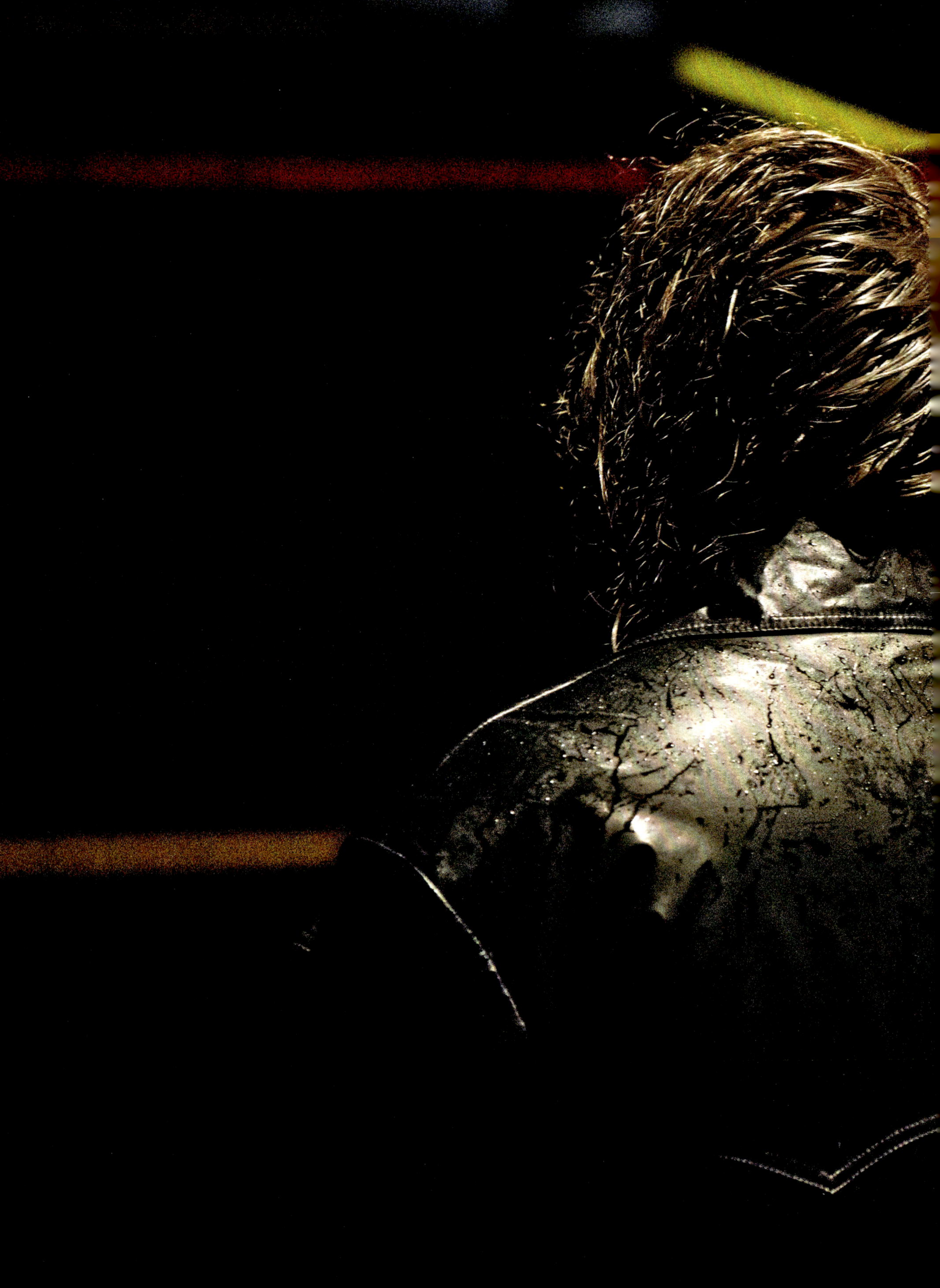

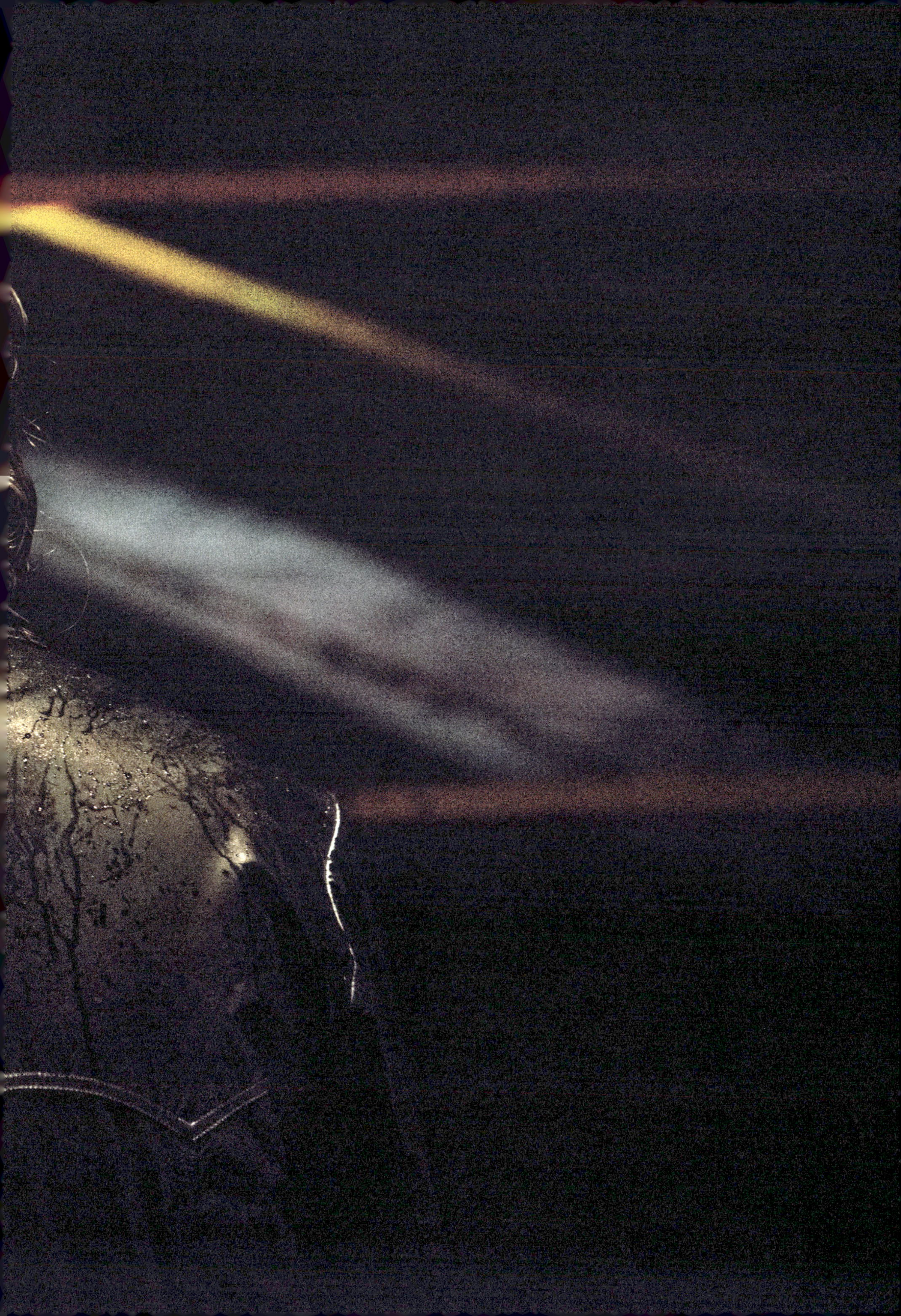

ARENA MURAL

2016
Latexdruck auf Vlies / Latex print on fleece
339 × 1036 cm

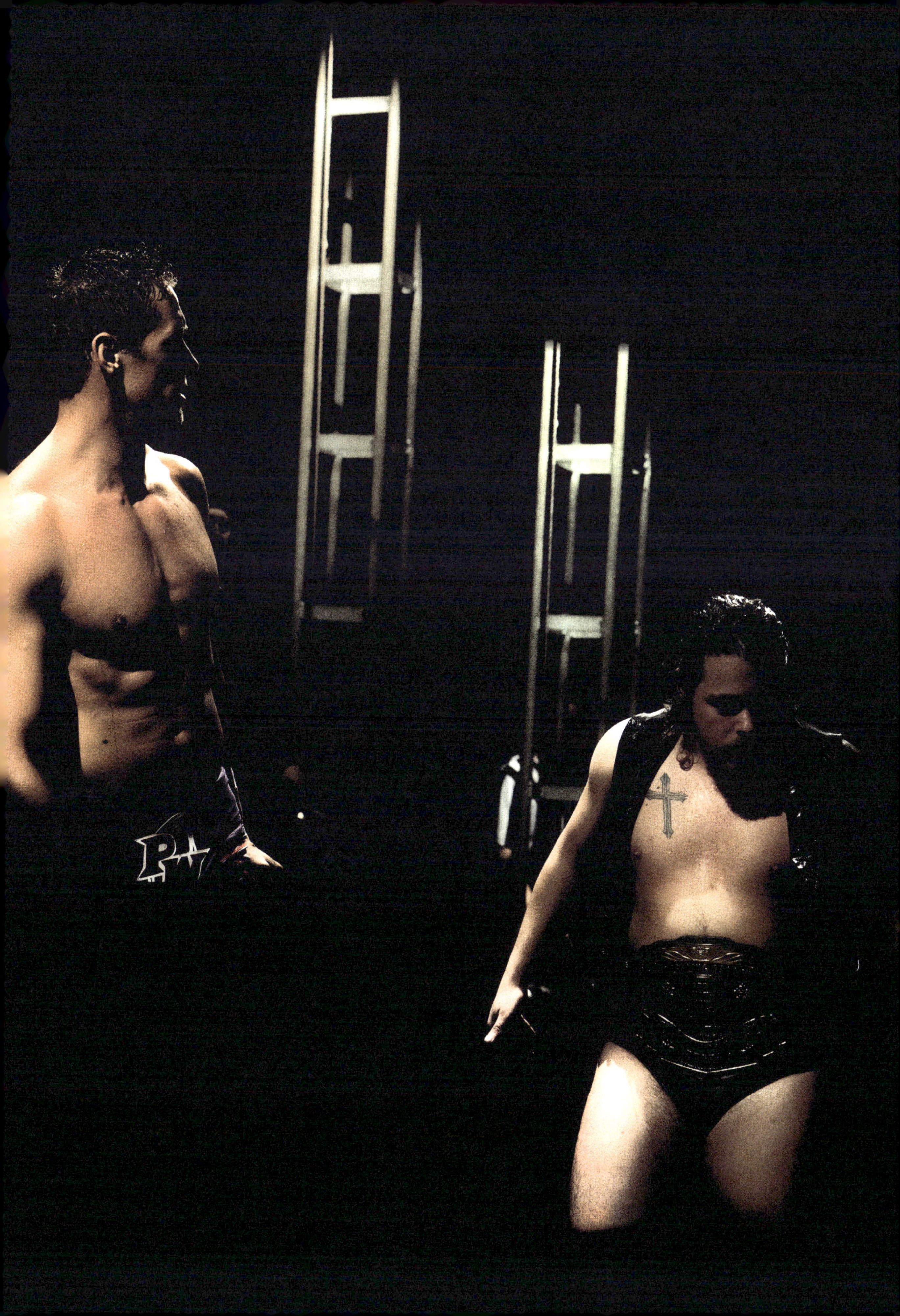

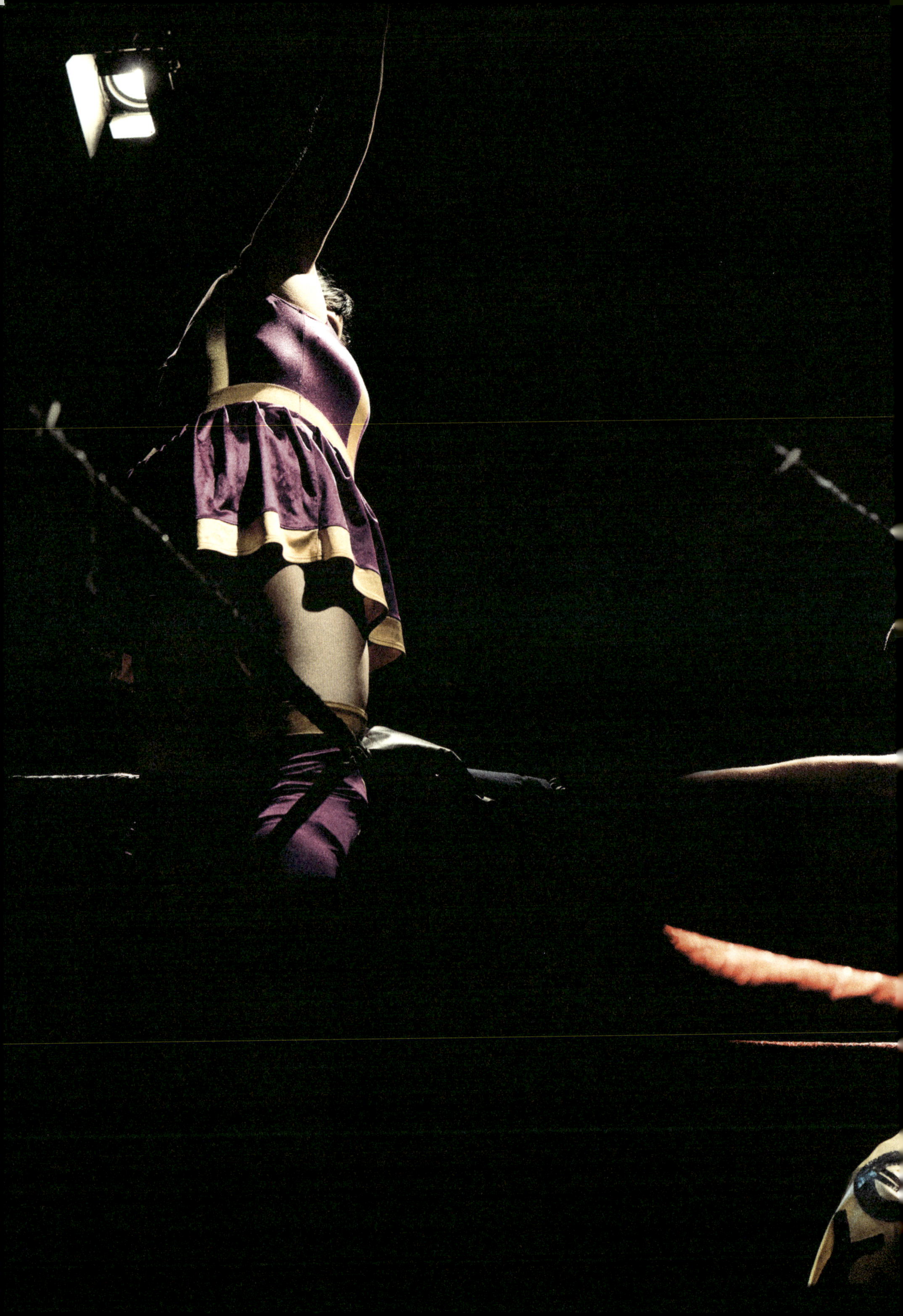

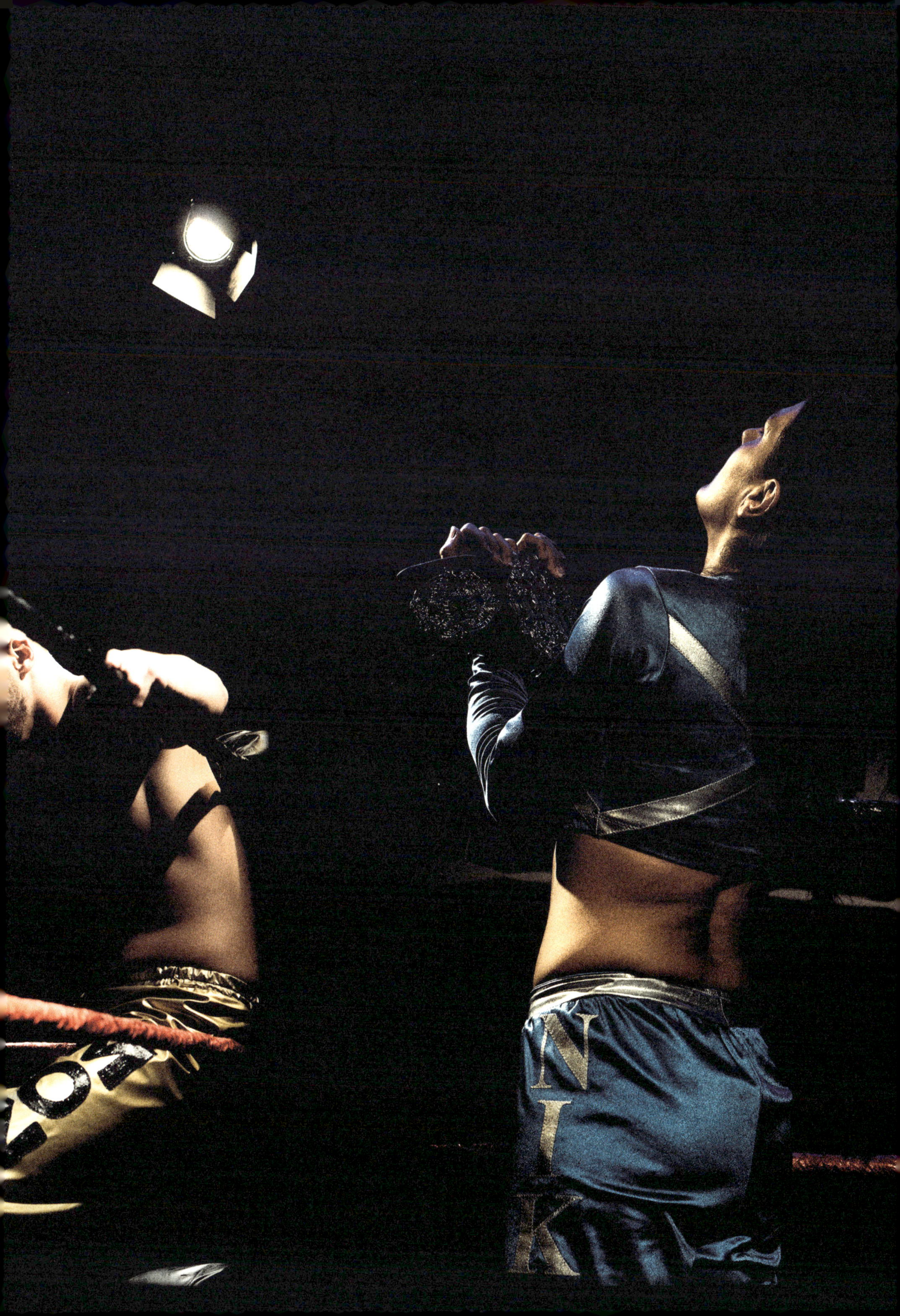
NIK

LOB DES SCHÖNSCHLAGENS. EIN CAPRICCIO

MICHAEL KOHTES

IN PRAISE OF BEAUTIFUL PUNCHING: A CAPRICCIO

MICHAEL KOHTES

Geben ist seliger denn Nehmen, pflegte mein alter Boxlehrer zu predigen. Womit er Sinn und Zweck der im Gym praktizierten Übungen auf den Begriff brachte: Zwar besteht die Kunst des Boxens primär darin, nicht getroffen zu werden, mithin Haken und Hiebe zu vermeiden, doch kennt der Heilsplan eines beherzten Faustfechters letztendlich nur ein Ziel – den Gegner gnadenlos und unwiderruflich niederzuschlagen, ihn ins Reich der Träume zu schicken. Welche Zerstörungskräfte dabei freigesetzt werden können, davon hat uns Mike Tyson, dieser fleischgewordene Albtraum aller Ringärzte, eine beklemmend plastische Vorstellung gegeben: »Ich versuche, die Nasenspitze meines Gegners zu treffen, ich will ihm das Nasenbein ins Gehirn treiben.«

Schöner wird so ein Gesicht davon nicht, gewiss. Indes führt das vom Kampf gezeichnete Antlitz eines Boxers uns immer auch die eigene Verwundbarkeit vor Augen – es erinnert daran, dass wir nicht zu Hause sind in unserem Körper. Wie dieser so oft geschmähte, weil angeblich brutale und primitive Sport ja überhaupt die destruktive, dunkle, unbewältigte Seite unserer Psyche hervorkehrt. Jeder Fight, den die Tiefstrahler aus dem Dunkel einer tobenden Arena schneiden, bricht mit einem der ältesten Tabus unserer Kultur: Du sollst nicht töten! Im »magischen Quadrat« feiert das fünfte Gebot die Ausnahme, hier darf der Mensch von seiner natürlichen Waffe, der Faust, hemmungsfrei Gebrauch machen, hier dürfen die unter dem Anpassungsdruck des Alltags gestauten Triebenergien, Kampf- und Angriffslust, bis zum Exzess, bis zum Knockout abventiliert werden. In dem Maß freilich, wie das Spektakel unsere Instinkte mobilisiert, offenbart sich zugleich, was Scham und Scheu zurückhalten: jenes Gewaltpotenzial, das sich eben auch abrupt entladen und dabei weiß Gott Schrecklicheres anrichten kann, als es ein Faustduell im Rahmen gültiger Regeln jemals könnte. Was das muskulös inszenierte Drama auf der Boxbühne spiegelt, ist das Drama der menschlichen Zivilisation, die allem Vernunfttraining zum Trotz von ihrer Idealform nur träumen kann. Einerseits.

Andererseits gewährt Boxen den Akteuren wie dem Publikum die Teilhabe an Erfahrungstiefen, die in archaischen Kulturen das Fest hervorrief. Jene rituellen, an heilige Orte und geweihte Fristen gebundenen Ausschweifungen, die allen Schauder, alle Scheu vor dem gewöhnlich Verbotenen in ihr Gegenteil verkehrten: die

More blessed are those who give than those who receive, my old boxing coach used to say. This described the essence of the exercises we practiced at the gym. Although the art of boxing is primarily about not getting hit, dodging hooks and uppercuts, a spirited fistfighter's hopes for salvation ultimately have only one goal: to mercilessly and irreversibly knock out the other man and send him to dreamland. A horrifically graphic idea of the destructive forces that can be released was described by Mike Tyson, the nightmare made flesh of every ringside doctor: "I try to catch him on the tip of his nose, because I try to punch the bone into his brain."

Certainly a face is not made prettier by this treatment. Yet a boxer's visage, bearing marks from fights, always makes visible our own vulnerability—reminding us that we are not at home in our bodies. This sport, so often maligned for supposedly being brutal and primitive, plumbs the depths of the destructive, dark, unresolved side of our psyche. Every fight, severed from the darkness of a roaring arena by the low-mounted spotlights, breaks one of the oldest taboos of our culture: Thou shalt not kill! In the "magic square" the fifth commandment celebrates an exception. Here a man may make uninhibited use of his natural weapon, the fist. Here the energies of our urges that have been pent up under the conformist pressures of everyday life, the desire to fight and attack, can be vented in excess, all the way up to the knock-out. To the same extent to which the spectacle mobilizes our instincts, it reveals what shame and timidity have held back: the potential for violence that can be abruptly unleashed and can, God knows, have worse consequences than a duel of fists subject to specific rules ever could. What the muscularly enacted drama on the boxing stage mirrors is the drama of human civilization, which, in spite of all the training of reason, can only dream of its ideal form. On the one hand.

On the other, boxing lets its protagonists and the audience take part in depths of experience called forth in archaic cultures by the festival, those ritual transgressions in holy places and for consecrated periods of time convert all shuddering and fear of what is conventionally forbidden into the opposite: the pleasure in breaking taboos. Wherever contempt for the taboo against killing is ceremonially celebrated, the will to sacrifice is aroused and human life is gambled with. Evil loses its terror and fear is revealed as desire, as a feverish longing that

Lust am Tabubruch. Wo die Missachtung des Tötungsverbots feierlich zelebriert, wo der Opferwille entfacht und das Leben aufs Spiel gesetzt wird, verliert das Böse seinen Schrecken, entpuppt sich die Angst als Begierde, als fieberhaftes Verlangen, das zur Ekstase sich steigert, wenn der gewaltsame Tod in spürbare Nähe rückt. Im kultischen Exzess kommen Wollust und Gräuel, Eros und Thanatos zur Deckung. Doch ist die Raserei nie grausamer als das Leben selbst; denn »was uns am heftigsten empört, ist in uns«, konstatiert der französische Denker Georges Bataille. Seinem Wesen nach sei das Leben selbst »ein Exzess, es ist Verschwendung von Leben«.

Sugar Ray Robinson, der so unvergleichlich boxte, wie Nijinsky tanzte, hat Gewalt, wie er beteuerte, nie gemocht. Folglich wollte er seinem Gegner auch gar nicht erst die Gelegenheit geben, »länger zwischen den Seilen zu bleiben, als für ihn gut sein könnte«. Natürlich ist Boxen heller Wahnsinn. Aber ein Wahnsinn mit Stil. »Die süße Kunst zu verletzen« erfordert Disziplin, Intelligenz und Können. Ein Boxer muss sich selbst erschaffen, er muss Bewegung und Punch in Einklang bringen, Schläge parieren und kombinieren, Tempo machen und Phantasie entwickeln. Ein blutiger Laie, wer in diesen komplexen Aktionen nur ein Walten kruder Kräfte sieht. Der Kampf mit den Fäusten lässt viel Raum für das Geniale, das Paradoxe und das Ungewisse. »In seinen intensivsten Momenten«, sekundiert uns die Autorin Joyce Carol Oates, sei Boxen »ein so ungebrochenes und so machtvolles Bild des Lebens – seiner Schönheit, seiner Verletzlichkeit und Verzweiflung, seines unberechenbaren und oft selbstzerstörerischen Muts –, dass es das Leben selbst ist und kaum ein bloßer Sport«.

Auch dies mag ein Grund dafür sein, dass den Schönschlägern von je die Herzen der Schöngeister zufliegen. Genau genommen schon seit den Tagen Homers, der den Pugilismus in die Poesie holte; siehe den sagenhaften Knockouter Epeios in der *Ilias.* Ob Pindar, Platon oder Plutarch: Was die faustkampfinspirierten Köpfe der Antike an den Muskelmännern faszinierte, waren die uralten Menschheitsgeschichten, die Geschichten vom Überleben und Sterben, die sich in den wilden, blutigen Begegnungen der Boxer extrem verdichteten – zu einer Dichtung in Aktion, voller Drastik und Dramatik. Diese Kunst war realistisch und magisch zugleich; eine Kunst, die vom Körper ausging und sich direkt auf den Körper bezog. Aufgeführt von archaischen Gestalten, die mit

intensifies into ecstasy when violent death comes palpably near. In cultic excess, lust and atrocity, Eros and Thanatos unite. Yet this franticness is never more cruel than life itself, for, as in the words of the French thinker Georges Bataille, "that which revolts us most violently is in us... Life in its essence is an excess, a prodigality of life."

Sugar Ray Robinson, who boxed as incomparably as Nijinsky danced, claimed he never liked violence. He joked that he didn't want to give his opponents the chance to stay in the ring longer than was good for them. Naturally boxing is sheer madness—but madness with style. "The sweet art of hurting" demands discipline, intelligence and ability. A boxer has to create himself, bringing motion and punch into harmony, has to parry and combine blows, has to set the pace and develop imagination. It is a very clueless layman who sees in these complex actions only the exercise of crude force. Fistfighting allows a great deal of space for genius, paradox and uncertainty. "At its moments of greatest intensity," the author Joyce Carol Oates concurs, boxing "seems to contain so complete and so powerful an image of life—life's beauty, vulnerability, despair, incalculable and often self-destructive courage—that boxing is life, and hardly a mere game."

This may be another reason for the fact that the hearts of aesthetes have long gone out to the beautiful punchers—at least since the days of Homer, who introduced pugilism into poetry with the legendary knock-out artist Epeius in the *Iliad.* Whether Pindar, Plato or Plutarch: the ancient minds inspired by fistfighting were fascinated by the prehistoric human stories, the stories of survival and death told in immensely condensed form in the boxers' wild, bloody meetings—a condensation in action, full of drastic dramatics. This art was at once realistic and magical, an art that emanated *from* the body and related directly *to* the body. It was performed by archaic figures who gripped the audience with the handwriting of their fists, scared and astonished them by releasing monstrous powers, defied all vulnerability and entered into those ecstatic regions "in which death is no longer the opposite of life" (Bataille).

No other sport so reliably distracts artists and writers from their work as does boxing. Some writers and artists tried it themselves: Lord Byron, George Bernard Shaw, Georges Braque, Ernest Hemingway, Miles Davis,

ihrer Faustschrift das Publikum wahrhaftig in Bann schlugen, es schaudern und staunen machten, da sie ungeheure Kräfte entfesselten, aller Verwundbarkeit trotzten und dabei in jene ekstatischen Regionen vordrangen, »wo der Tod nicht mehr der Gegensatz des Lebens ist« (Bataille).

Von keiner zweiten Sportart lassen sich Künstler und Schriftsteller so zuverlässig aus der Arbeitsröhre locken wie vom Boxen. Darunter etliche, die selbst damit anfingen: Lord Byron, Shaw, Braque, Hemingway, Miles Davis, Sartre, ja, auch dieser Bleistiftathlet... Und alle machte das Fäusteschwingen auf eine je eigene Weise schlauer. Der Theaterpraktiker Fritz Kortner, der bei Max Schmeling Boxstunden nahm und mit seinen Berliner Sportsfreunden Brecht und Grosz die Großkampftage besuchte, schärfte an den Faustfechtern seinen Blick für Theatralik, für Gestik und Mimik. »Von der sportlichen Faszination abgesehen«, schreibt er in seinen Memoiren, »fesselte mich der Zweikampf als Drama. Die Ausdrucksskala in Gesicht, Augen und Körper des Boxers war für mich eine erregende und anregende Lehrstunde.«

Sobald ein Boxer in den Ring steigt, ist er der einsamste Mensch der Welt. Unter den Augen der Menge stellt er sich einer Situation, mit der er allein fertig werden muss. Ein Boxer kann sich weder verstecken, noch kann er davonlaufen; alles, was er in diesem gottverlassenen Seilgeviert tun kann, ist, sein Schicksal in beide Fäuste zu nehmen und zu versuchen, das Beste daraus zu machen. Boxen heißt, sich auf eine Auseinandersetzung einzulassen, die den Existenzkampf, und zwar in seiner ganzen Härte, auf ein Dutzend Runden komprimiert: einstecken und austeilen, sich nicht aufgeben, sondern gegenhalten, mit Finten und Tricks, ohne Nerven zu zeigen und ohne sich in seinem Handeln beirren zu lassen; dabei stets die Gefahr im Nacken, dass mit einem Schlag buchstäblich alles vorbei sein könnte. Wie im Boxring, also auch auf Erden. Man versucht, eine gute Figur zu machen, und kämpft, bis man nicht mehr kann. Und was hat man am Ende davon?

Siege sind, wie jeder Boxer weiß, nur eine Pause zwischen zwei Leiden. Wer das Seilviereck als Gewinner verlässt, erntet Anerkennung, Lorbeer, Ruhm, Reichtum. Doch geht der gewonnene Fight dem nächsten voraus, womit das selbstgewählte Schicksal von Neuem die

Jean-Paul Sartre—yes, even that pencil athlete, too. And throwing punches made all of them smarter in their own different ways. The theater practitioner Fritz Kortner, who took boxing lessons from Max Schmeling and went to the big matches with his fellow Berlin sports fans Bertolt Brecht and George Grosz, watched fistfighters to sharpen his eye for theatricality, gesture and facial expression. "Apart from the athletic fascination," he wrote in his memoirs, "I was captivated by the fight as a drama. The scale of expressions in the face, eyes and body of the boxer were an exciting and inspiring lesson for me."

When a boxer goes into the ring, he is the loneliest man in the world. Under the eyes of the crowd, he faces a situation that he must deal with by himself. A boxer cannot hide or run; all he can do in this god-forsaken roped-off quadrangle is to take his fate in both fists and try to make the best of it. Boxing means agreeing to a confrontation that is a struggle for survival in all its toughness, comprising twelve rounds: getting in and hitting hard, not giving up but holding up, using feints and tricks, not showing nerves and not letting oneself get confused in one's actions, dogged all the while by the fear that everything could be over with one punch. As in the boxing ring, so on earth. One tries to cut a good figure, and one fights till one can't fight any longer. And what does one get from it in the end?

Victories, as every boxer knows, are only an intermission between sufferings. The person who leaves the ropes as the victor wins recognition, laurels, fame, riches. Yet the fight that has been won precedes the next fight, and the self-chosen fate demands going back to the grind, the struggle against oneself, the strict, monotonous monk's existence, secluded from the temptations and influences of the outside world, knowing that boxing usually "goes through the head" (Manfred Wolke), and that a fight is decided not only in the space of the twelve rounds, sometimes as short as 40 seconds each, but in particular in the preceding weeks and months of self-denial. So much the better if these labors are not in vain, if, indeed, lasting success arrives. But as the shooting star George Foreman said (after he had gotten used to the glamour), you have to get to know defeat before you can appreciate victory.

What a loser can win was seen in Hamburg in 2003, when Dariusz Michalczewski, known as "the Tiger," lost the light heavyweight title to the Mexican boxer Julio

Schinderei befiehlt, den Kampf gegen sich selbst, das strenge, monotone Mönchsleben, abgekapselt von den Lockrufen und Einflüssen der Umwelt, wissend, dass Boxen hauptsächlich »durch den Kopf geht« (Manfred Wolke) und dass ein Wettkampf nicht nur über die Zwölf-Runden-Distanz, die mitunter kurze 40 Sekunden lang sein kann, entschieden wird, sondern vor allem in den Wochen und Monaten der Selbstkasteiung. Umso erfreulicher, wenn sie nicht vergeblich war, ja womöglich sogar dauerhafter Erfolg sich einstellt. Doch wie wusste der Shootingstar George Foreman, nachdem er sich an den Glamour gewöhnt hatte: »Man muss die Niederlage kennengelernt haben, bevor man den Sieg zu schätzen weiß.«

Was derweil ein Verlierer zu gewinnen vermag, das konnte man 2003 in Hamburg sehen, als Dariusz Michalczewski, der »Tiger«, nach 48 Siegen in Serie die Krone im Halbschwergewicht an den Mexikaner Gonzalez verlor. Die Entscheidung der Punktrichter war streitbar knapp. Das Publikum maulte und pfiff. Der Tiger aber blieb ruhig, er fauchte nicht und er jaulte nicht, sondern ging zu Gonzalez, verbeugte sich und reichte ihm die Hand zur Gratulation. In diesem Moment gewann der Tiger mehr als in allen Ringschlachten zuvor – menschliche Größe.

Boxen ist ein männliches Refugium. Mithin fänden weibliche Zuschauer hier reichlich Gelegenheit, der Innenwelt des Mannes ansichtig zu werden. Rocky Graziano, das amerikanische Einwandereridol, verkörperte den Machismo in Reinkultur, dieser Wildling kannte im Ring nur ein Ziel: »meinen Gegner notfalls auch zu ermorden«. Doch kaum war die letzte Runde ausgefochten, offenbarte er den Blicken der Menge das Tiefste, was eine Boxerseele besitzt – die Zärtlichkeit, die sie für ihren Rivalen empfindet. Graziano pflegte seine Gegner nach dem Kampf zu küssen. Er umarmte und er küsste sie. So, als hätte sich im Verlauf des martialischen Gefechts, irgendwo auf der Schwelle zwischen Clinch und Todesnähe, das Gefühl eines fatalen Miteinanders eingestellt, die Erkenntnis einer gemeisamen Verdammnis, aus der jene Sympathie zu erwachsen schien, die nach dem erlösenden Schlussgong in der brüderlichen Umarmung ihren intimsten und gleichzeitig unbefangensten Ausdruck fand. Dankbarkeit, Respekt und Zuneigung lagen in dieser menschlichen Geste, als hätte es tatsächlich erst der leidenschaftlichen Tortur und

César Gonzalez after 48 straight victories. The decision by the scoring judge was controversially close. The audience booed and whistled. But the Tiger kept his calm, he did not hiss or yowl, he went over to Gonzalez, bowed down and extended a hand in congratulation. In this moment, the Tiger won more than in all his previous victories in the ring combined: human greatness.

Boxing is a male refuge. Female spectators can find an abundance of opportunities here to observe men's inner world. Rocky Graziano, the idol of American immigrants, embodied pure machismo, a wild animal with tunnel vision in the ring, saying of an opponent: "I wanted to kill him. I like him but I wanted to kill him." Yet no sooner was the last round fought than Graziano gave the watching crowd a revelation of the deepest thing a boxer's soul possesses—the feeling of tenderness for a rival. Graziano would often kiss his opponents after a fight. He embraced them and kissed them. As though, over the course of the martial encounter, somewhere on the threshold between the clinch and the nearness of death, a feeling began of a fatal togetherness, the recognition of a shared damnation, seemingly growing out of that sympathy that, after the salvation of the final gong, found its most intimate and uninhibited expression in the fraternal embrace. Gratitude, respect and affection were contained in this human gesture, as though passionate torture and a rivalry taken to the extreme were necessary to break through the armor of isolation and open one up to another man. Is it conceivable that the real attraction of this brutish fighting sport is not destruction at all, but understanding?

If the essence of passion is to replace the unbearable "discontinuity" of individuals who exist separately from one another with "a miraculous continuity between two beings," as our informant Bataille believes, then surely the passion of boxing, too, can be motivated in essence by the aspiration for the dissolution of boundaries, that is, communication—that genuine, wordless form of understanding that can succeed only in moments outside of the self. "'Communication,'" Bataille writes, "requires individuals whose separate existence in themselves is risked, placed at the limit of death and nothingness."

If a man who loses a title succeeds in returning to the ring, he can become more than just a world champion. He has a chance at boxing himself into the Olympus of true champs, attained only by those men who defy the worst

einer bis zum Äußersten getriebenen Rivalität bedurft, um den Panzer der Isolation zu durchbrechen und sich füreinander zu öffnen. Wäre es demnach denkbar, dass der eigentliche Reiz dieses brachialen Kampfspiels gar nicht in der Vernichtung, sondern in der Verständigung liegt?

Wenn es das Wesen der Leidenschaft ist, die unerträgliche »Diskontinuität« der voneinander getrennt existierenden Individuen durch »eine wunderbare Kontinuität zwischen zwei Wesen« zu ersetzen, wie unser Gewährsmann Bataille meint, dann dürfte zweifellos auch die Passion des Boxens wesentlich durch die Aussicht auf Entgrenzung, sprich: Kommunikation motiviert sein – jene genuine, wortlose Form der Verständigung, wie sie eben nur in den Momenten des Außer-sich-Seins gelingen kann: »Die ›Kommunikation‹ findet nur *zwischen zwei aufs Spiel gesetzten Wesen* statt – zerrissen in der Schwebe, beide über ihr Nichts gebeugt.«

Gelingt es einem Titelverlierer noch einmal, in den Ring zurückzukehren, kann er mehr werden als bloß Weltmeister. Er hat die Chance, sich in den Olymp der wahren Champs zu boxen, wohin nur diejenigen gelangen, die den bösesten aller Flüche, die auf dem Boxsport lasten, durchbrechen: *They never come back.* Weltmeister, die ungeschlagen abtreten, wie die Knockout-Maschine Rocky Marciano (nicht zu verwechseln mit Graziano), der in 49 Kämpfen nicht ein einziges Mal unterlegen war, werden bestenfalls bestaunt, aber nicht bewundert. Was ihnen fehlt, ist die Aura ebenjener Boxkünstler, die erst vernichtet werden müssen, um sich dann mit einem triumphalen Comeback unsterblich zu machen.

Floyd Patterson wurde unsterblich, nachdem er die Schmach, die ihm der Außenseiter Ingemar Johansson zugefügt hatte, im Rematch durch einen spektakulären K.-o.-Sieg wettmachte und sich damit als erster Weltmeister aller Klassen den Titel zurückholte. Später waren es Ausnahmeathleten vom Schlag eines Lennox Lewis, die das Wunder der Wiederkehr vollbrachten. Auch Lewis wähnte sich schon auf dem Weg zur Unschlagbarkeit, als ihn 2001 wie aus heiterem Himmel die krachende Rechte von Hasim Rahman traf. Blamiert bis auf die Knochen, musste der selbsternannte *Mister Jekyll and Mister Hyde* erst einmal seine Selbstzweifel bezwingen, bevor er bei der Revanche seinen Widersacher mit einer Salve furioser Wirkungstreffer aus dem Viereck fegte.

of all curses leveled at the sport of boxing: "They never come back." World champions who retire undefeated, like the knock-out machine Rocky Marciano (not to be confused with Graziano), who did not lose a single time in 49 fights, are at best marveled at, not admired. What they lack is the aura of those boxing artists who must first be annihilated so as to then become immortal through a triumphal comeback.

Floyd Patterson, after his defeat by the outsider Ingemar Johansson, became immortal by making good with a spectacular KO win in a rematch, regaining the title and becoming the first world champion in every weight class. Later, exceptional athletes like Lennox Lewis worked the wonder of a comeback. Lewis himself imagined he was already on the road to invincibility when in 2001 Hasim Rahman landed a smashing punch like a bolt from the blue. Embarrassed to the bone, the self-proclaimed "Mister Jekyll and Mister Hyde" had to overcome his self-doubt before he could face a rematch and drive his opponent from the ring with a furious salvo of hard jabs and hooks.

The comeback king par excellence, of course, is and always will be Muhammad Ali, the boxing "enfant flexible." Thanks to a versatile style paired with a simply incredible force of will, "the Greatest" proved no fewer than three times that he would not be made small. The first time came after his forced retirement for refusing the draft ("I ain't got no quarrel with the Vietcong"), when he put Jerry Quarry to sleep in Atlanta. Four years later, at the legendary "Rumble in the Jungle" in 1974, he reclaimed the WBA and WBC titles with a KO win against the 220-pound colossus George Foreman. And finally Leon Spinks, too, had to acknowledge that no man could dethrone "America's biggest ego" (as Ali was glorified by his tireless promoter Norman Mailer) without paying the price. With the lesson that Ali taught him in the rematch, Spinks was to realize the bitter truth that only the giants can disprove: "They never come back."

Fate catches up with everyone sooner or later. At some point every boxer, even an Ali, fights against growing old, against fatigue and time running away from him. Time runs away from every athlete, but no athlete ages more quickly and visibly than a fistfighter. Assuming the martyrdom of a boxing career means inexorably hauling out everything, really everything, that there is in a man's body—to say nothing of the psychic strain. A fighter can endure an

Der Comeback-König par excellence ist und bleibt natürlich Muhammad Ali. Das boxende Enfant flexible. Dank seines wandlungsfähigen Stils, gepaart mit einer schier unglaublichen Willenskraft, bewies »der Größte« gleich dreimal, dass er nicht kleinzukriegen war: erstmals nach seiner Zwangspause wegen Kriegsdienstverweigerung (»I ain't got no quarrel with the Viet Cong«), als er in Atlanta Jerry Quarry in den Tiefschlaf versetzte. Vier Jahre später, 1974 beim legendären *Rumble in the Jungle*, holte er sich durch seinen K.-o.-Triumph über den 220-Pfund-Koloss George Foreman die Trophäen der WBA und WBC zurück. Und schließlich musste auch Leon Spinks einsehen, dass man »Amerikas größtes Ego«, wie ihn sein unermüdlicher Herold Norman Mailer verherrlichte, nicht ungestraft vom Thron stößt. Mit der Lektion, die ihm Ali beim Rückkampf erteilte, sollte sich für Spinks jene bittere Wahrheit erfüllen, die zu widerlegen eben nur den Giganten gegeben ist – *They never come back.*

Früher oder später ereilt jeden das Schicksal. Denn irgendwann kämpft jeder Boxer, selbst ein Ali, gegen das Älterwerden, die Müdigkeit und die Zeit, die ihm davonläuft. Allen Athleten läuft sie davon, doch keiner altert schneller und sichtbarer als ein Faustkämpfer. Das Martyrium einer Boxkarriere auf sich zu nehmen bedeutet unweigerlich, alles, wirklich alles aus seinem Körper herauszuholen. Von den psychischen Strapazen gar nicht zu reden. Körperlichen Schmerz kann ein Fighter erstaunlich gut aushalten; was ihm mehr zusetzt, ist die Vorstellung, dass der nächste Kampf zugleich sein letzter sein könnte. Wer durch das Fegefeuer der Fäuste geht, riskiert ja mehr als nur eine Niederlage – er riskiert sich selbst. Wobei die Angst zu scheitern in dem Maße wächst, wie Erwartungs- und Erfolgsdruck zunehmen. In keiner Branche liegen Aufstieg und Fall so dicht beieinander, sind die Gipfel des Ruhms so abschüssig wie in der Welt des Profiboxens.

Fast alle großen Champs kamen aus dem Nichts und kehrten ins Nichts zurück. Joe Louis saß im Rollstuhl, nachdem ihn Schulden, Psychosen und Kokainsucht aufgefressen hatten. Sonny Liston war achtunddreißig, als er unter dubiosen Umständen an einer Überdosis Heroin starb. Panama Al Brown, dessen elegante, gestochene Faustschrift das Publikum zu Beifallsstürmen hingerissen hatte, vegetierte zuletzt in den Verliererstraßen von New York, hauptberuflich als Tellerwäscher, er endete im Armenspital. Für den italienischen Boxstar Anacleto Locatelli, Europas Nummer eins im Leichtgewicht, war

astonishing amount of physical pain; what preys on him more is the thought that the next fight could be his last. He who goes through the purgatory of fists risks more than just a defeat; he risks himself. The fear of failure increases alongside the growing pressure of expectations and success. In no other profession are rise and fall so close together; nor does the peak of fame slope so steeply downward, as in the world of professional boxing.

Nearly every great champ came from nothing and went back to nothing. Joe Louis was left in a wheelchair, having been eaten up by debts, psychoses and his cocaine addiction. Sonny Liston was 38 years old when he died from an overdose of heroin under questionable circumstances. Panama Al Brown, the elegant, precise handwriting of whose fists had won storms of applause from enraptured audiences, wasted away in poverty in New York, for the most part working as a dishwasher and died in a charity hospital. Living under the bridges of Paris was the final station for the Italian star boxer Anacleto Locatelli. He had been the number one lightweight in Europe, and he died homeless. "The bigger they come, the harder they fall." This is the fatal dialectic of a sport that produces more material for tragedies than any other.

Panama Al Brown, the *pugiliste maudit*, was a genius bantamweight who proved how the art of boxing can merge into great art. His protégé for a time, the poet Jean Cocteau, wanted a "muscular spirit" and fell in love with the poetry of fistfighting. Artists of boxing and poetry, wrote the "paperweight" athlete, had some things in common: "We use what the public would call the same tricks." For his part, the Spanish painter Eduardo Arroyo, who explored the rites of boxing with an ethnological gaze and saw himself in the fistworkers' battles, wrote a biography of Al Brown. In these ways the fine arts permeated one another in the arena of Modernism. When the avant-gardes thumbed their noses at the old canon of the muses and inquired into the conditions of our earthly existence, the boundary dissolved between the salon and the street, between art and life. Not the final work, but the creative impetus, not an action's morality but its elegance became criteria of artistic individuality. It followed that the outlandish handwriting of a boxer's fists could itself receive the holy orders of the artistically beautiful.

I once asked my old boxing coach how he fell for boxing, of all things. He had been a passable puncher himself in his youth and had had some famous sparring

unter den Brücken von Paris Endstation Sehnsucht – er starb als Clochard. *The bigger they come, the harder they fall.* Das ist die fatale Dialektik einer Sportart, die mehr Stoff für Tragödien produziert als jede andere.

Panama Al Brown, der *pugiliste maudit*, hatte als Bantamgenie bewiesen, wie die Boxkunst mit der großen Kunst verschmelzen kann; sein zeitweiliger Protegé, der Dichter Jean Cocteau, wollte ausschließlich seinen »Geist muskulös haben« und verliebte sich in die Poesie des Faustfechtens; Box- und Dichtkünstler, so der Papiergewichtler, hätten manches gemeinsam: »Wir wenden an, was die Menge *die gleichen Tricks* nennen würde.« Der spanische Maler Eduardo Arroyo wiederum, der mit ethnologischem Blick die Riten des Boxens erforschte und sich in den Kämpfen der Faustwerker wiedererkannte, schrieb eine Biografie über Al Brown. Dieserart durchdrangen sich in der Arena der Moderne die schönen Künste gegenseitig. Seitdem die Avantgarden auf den alten Musenkanon pfiffen und nach den Bedingungen unserer irdischen Existenz fragten, waren die Grenzen zwischen Salon und Straße, Kunst und Leben offen. Nicht das abgeschlossene Werk, sondern der schöpferische Impetus, nicht die Moral, sondern die Eleganz einer Tat wurden zu Kriterien künstlerischer Individualität. Folglich konnte auch die ausgefallene Faustschrift eines Boxers die höheren Weihen des Kunstschönen erhalten.

Warum er ausgerechnet dem Boxen verfallen sei, fragte ich meinen alten Boxlehrer, der früher, in seiner Jugend, selbst ein passabler Puncher war, sogar mit etlichen Berühmtheiten gesparrt hatte. Keine Ahnung, sagte er, was soll ich dazu sagen, aber der Marvin Hagler (das Mittelgewichts-Ass der Achtzigerjahre), der habe mal einen schönen Satz losgelassen: »Wenn man irgendwann meinen Schädel aufschneidet, wird man darin einen großen Boxhandschuh finden. Das ist alles, was ich bin. Es ist mein Leben.«

partners. No idea, he said, what should I say? But, he said, Marvin Hagler (the middleweight wonder of the 1980s) once had a good line: "If they cut my bald head open, they'll find one big boxing glove inside. That's all I am. I live it."

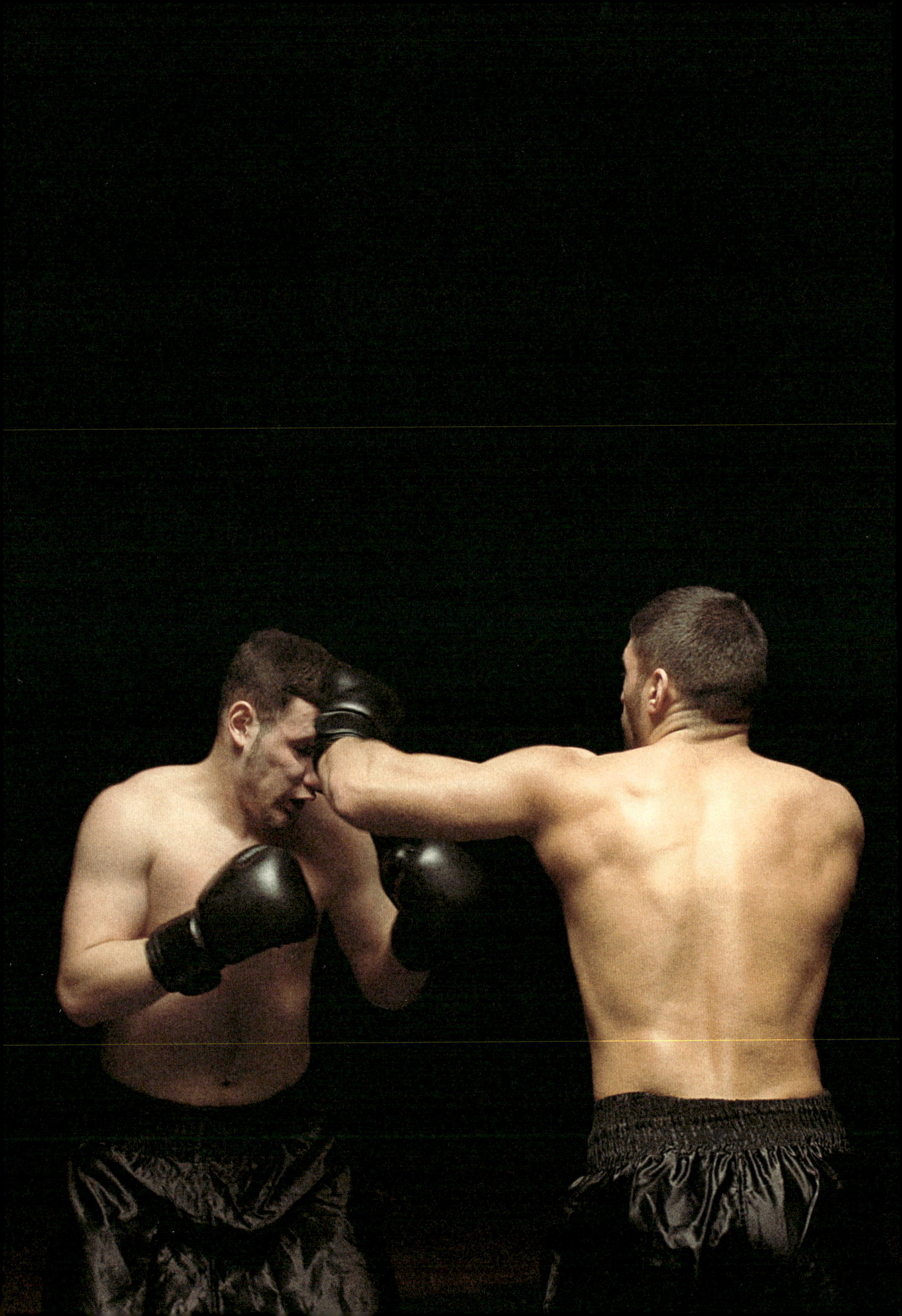

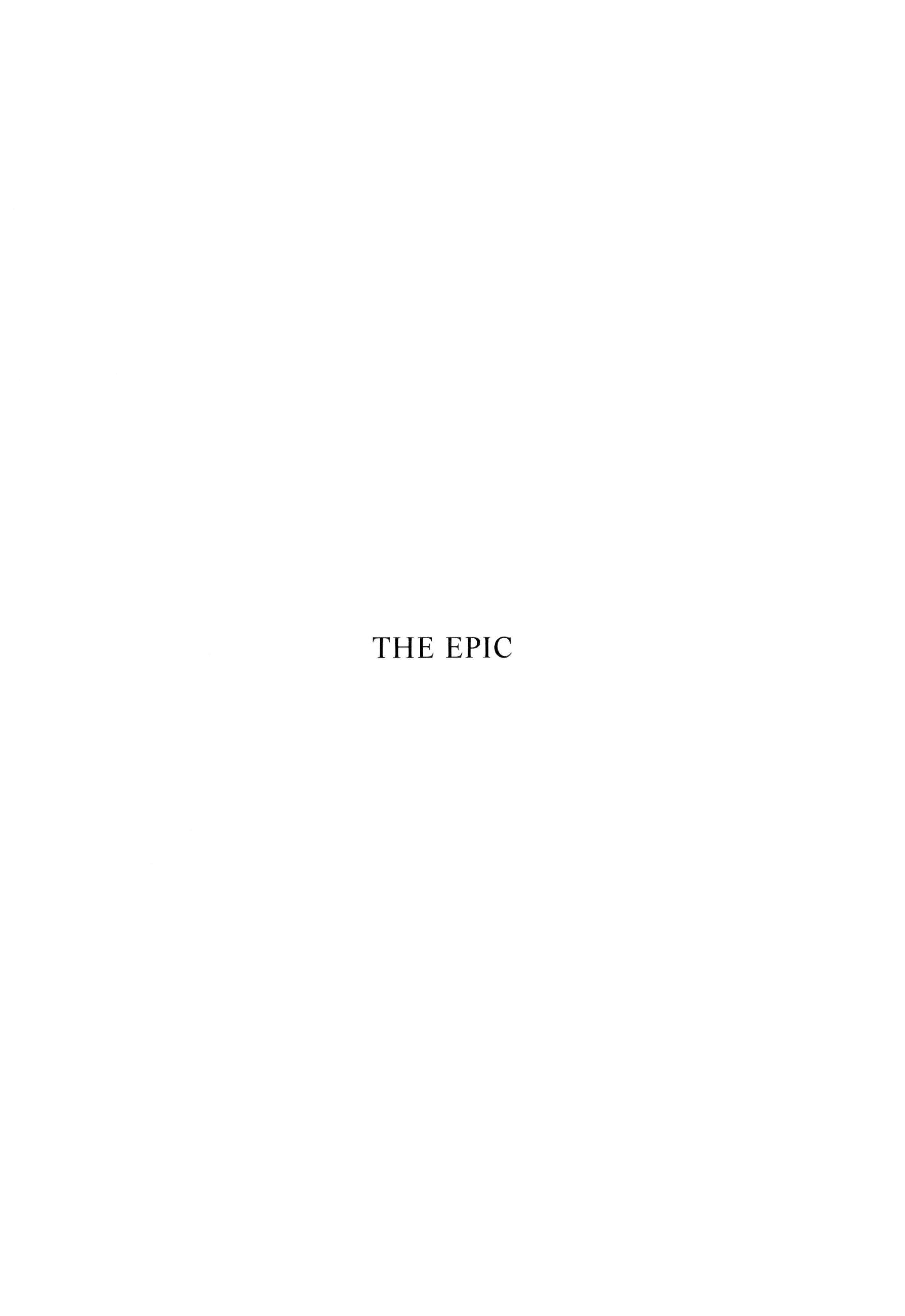

THE EPIC

THE EPIC

2016
HD Video, 24'14", Sound

Ein Film von / A film by
Pola Sieverding

Mit / With
Abdullah Karalioglu, Azamat Machmudov

Kamera / Camera
Christoph Manz

Soundtrack
Orson Sieverding

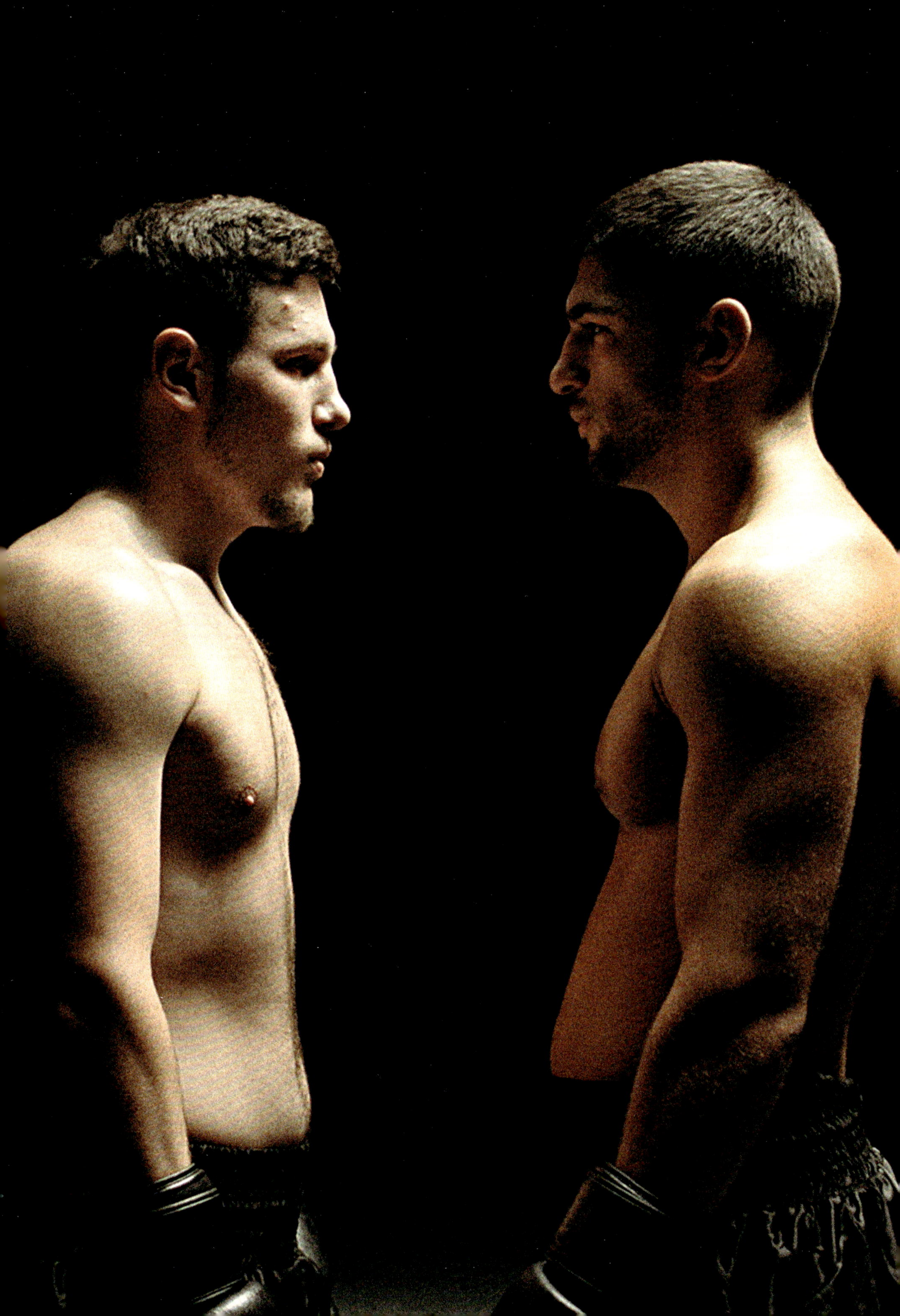

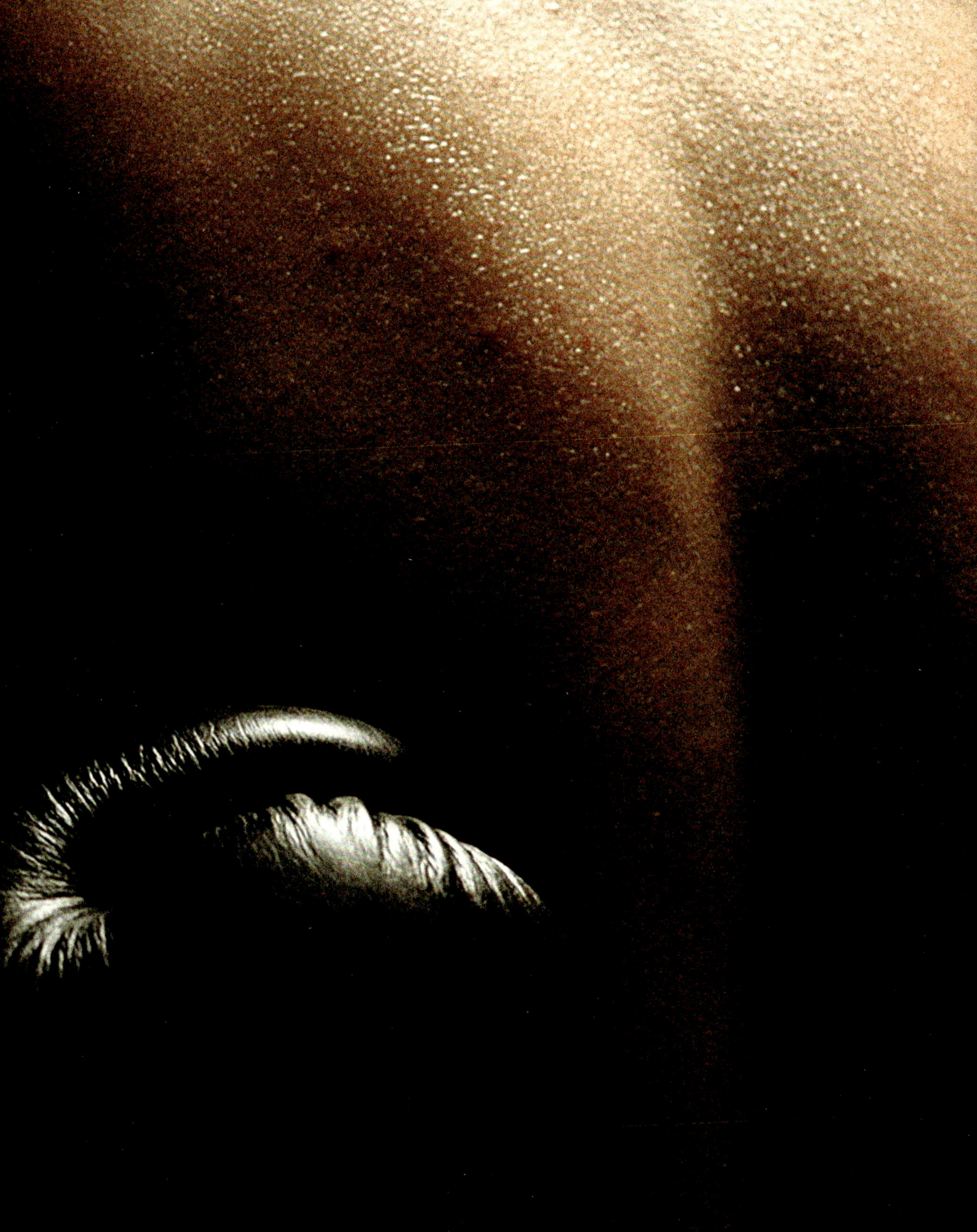

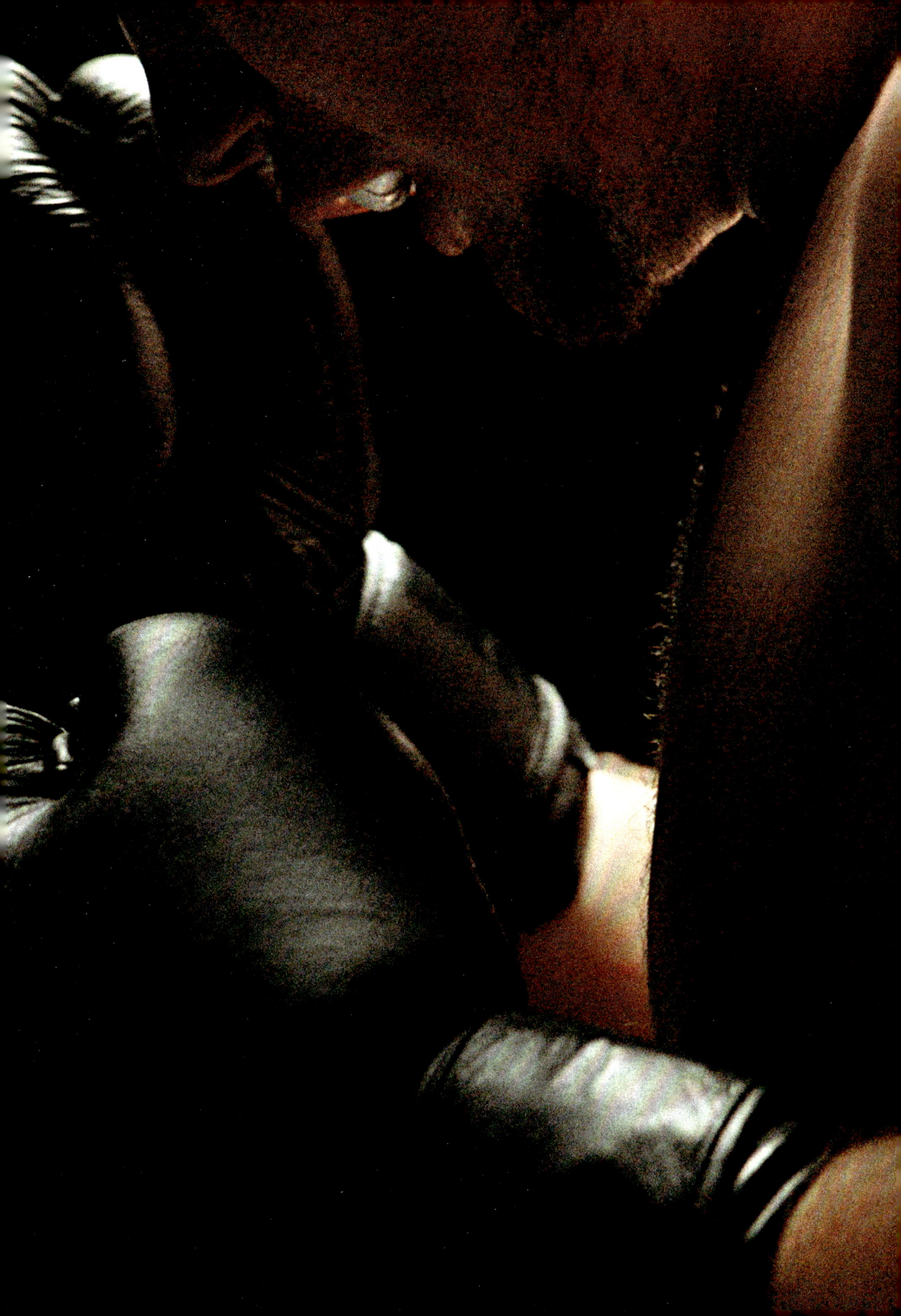

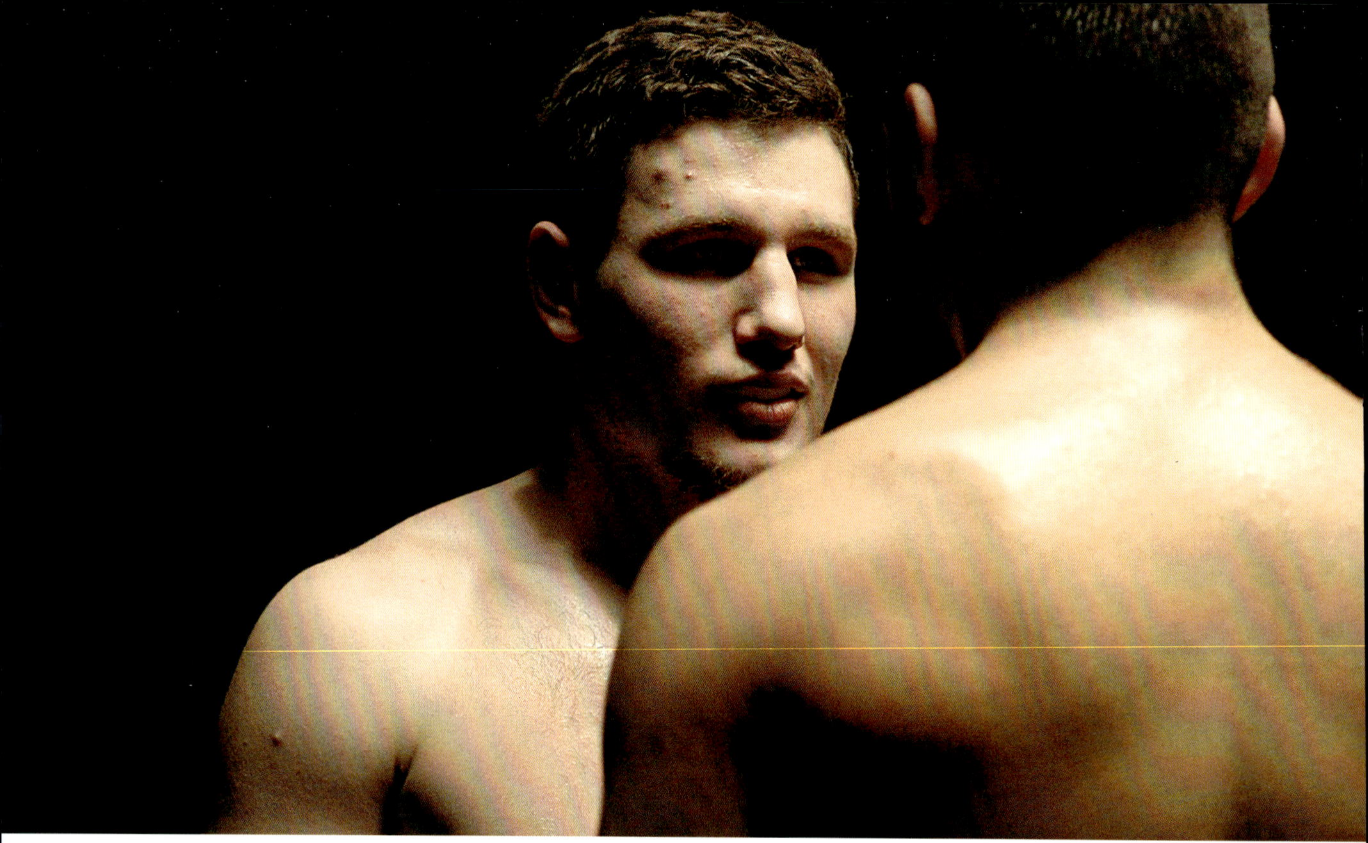

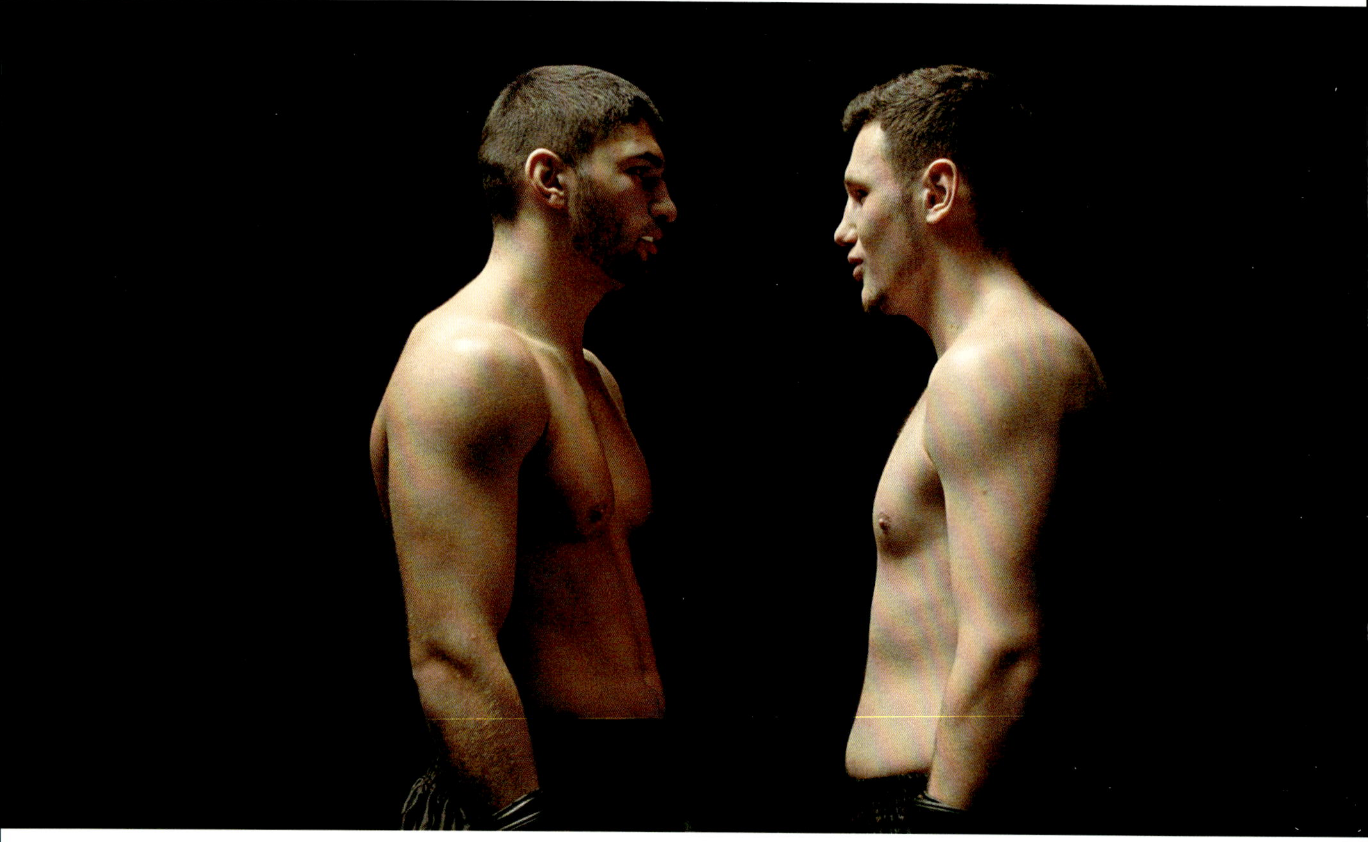

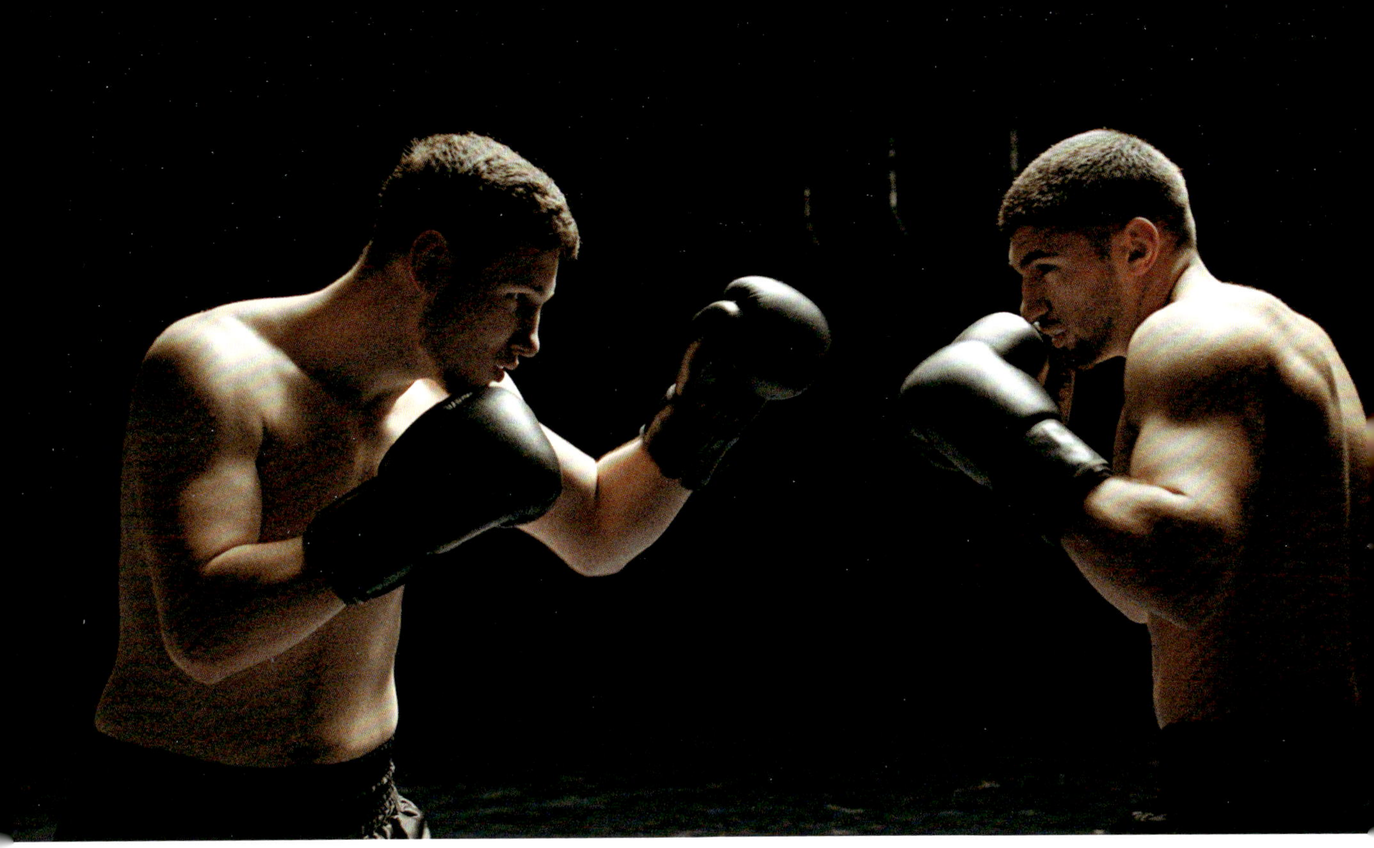

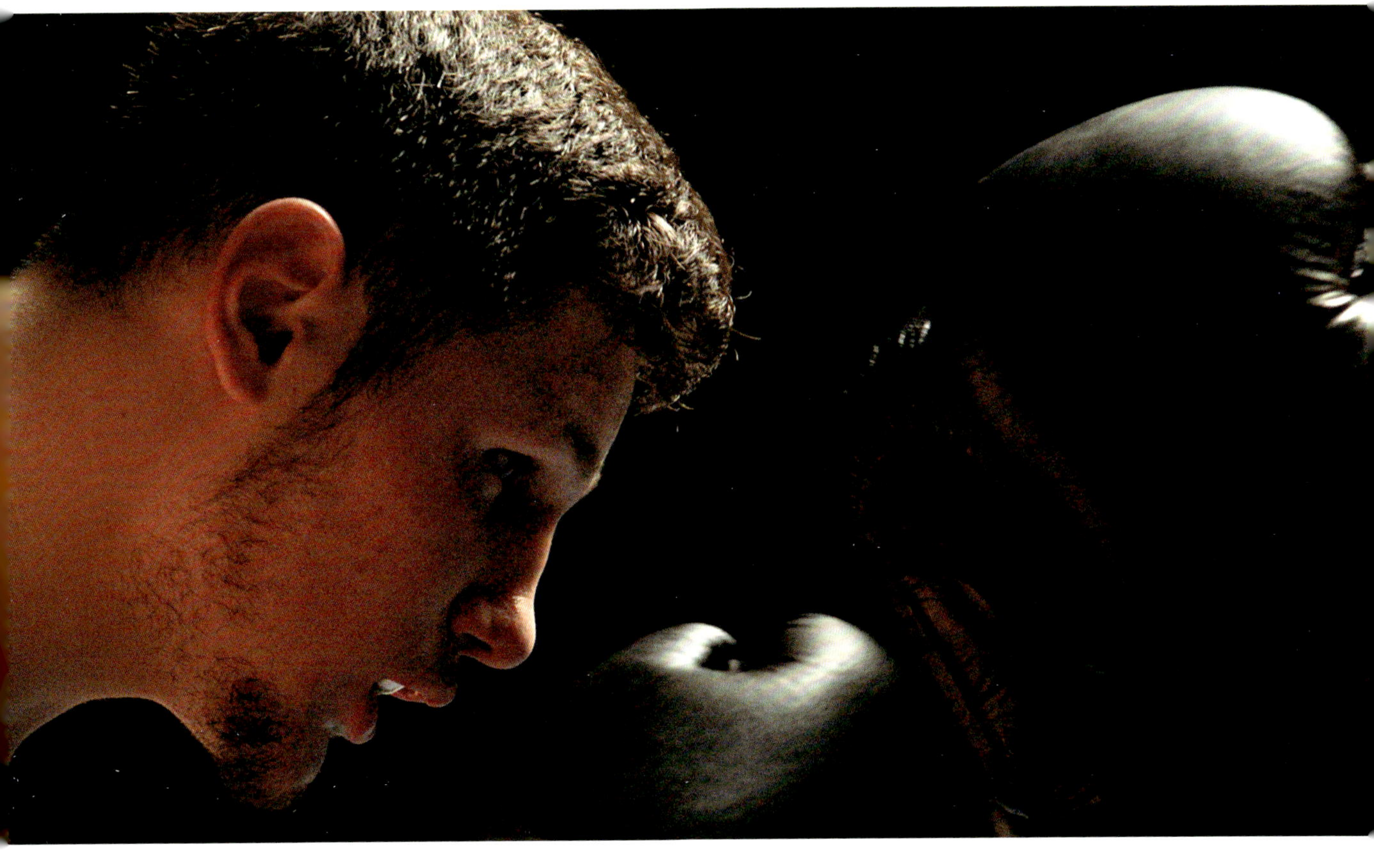

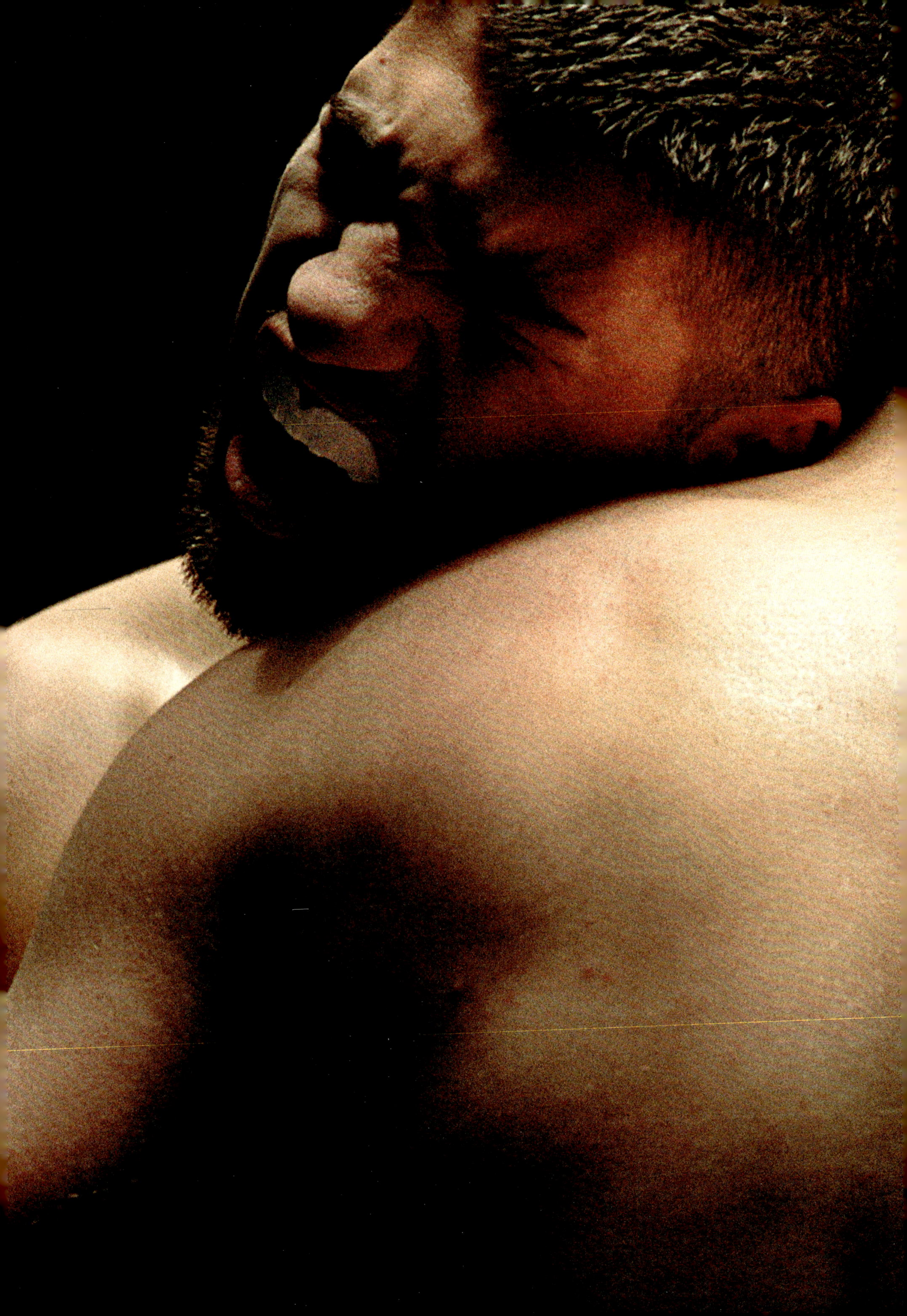

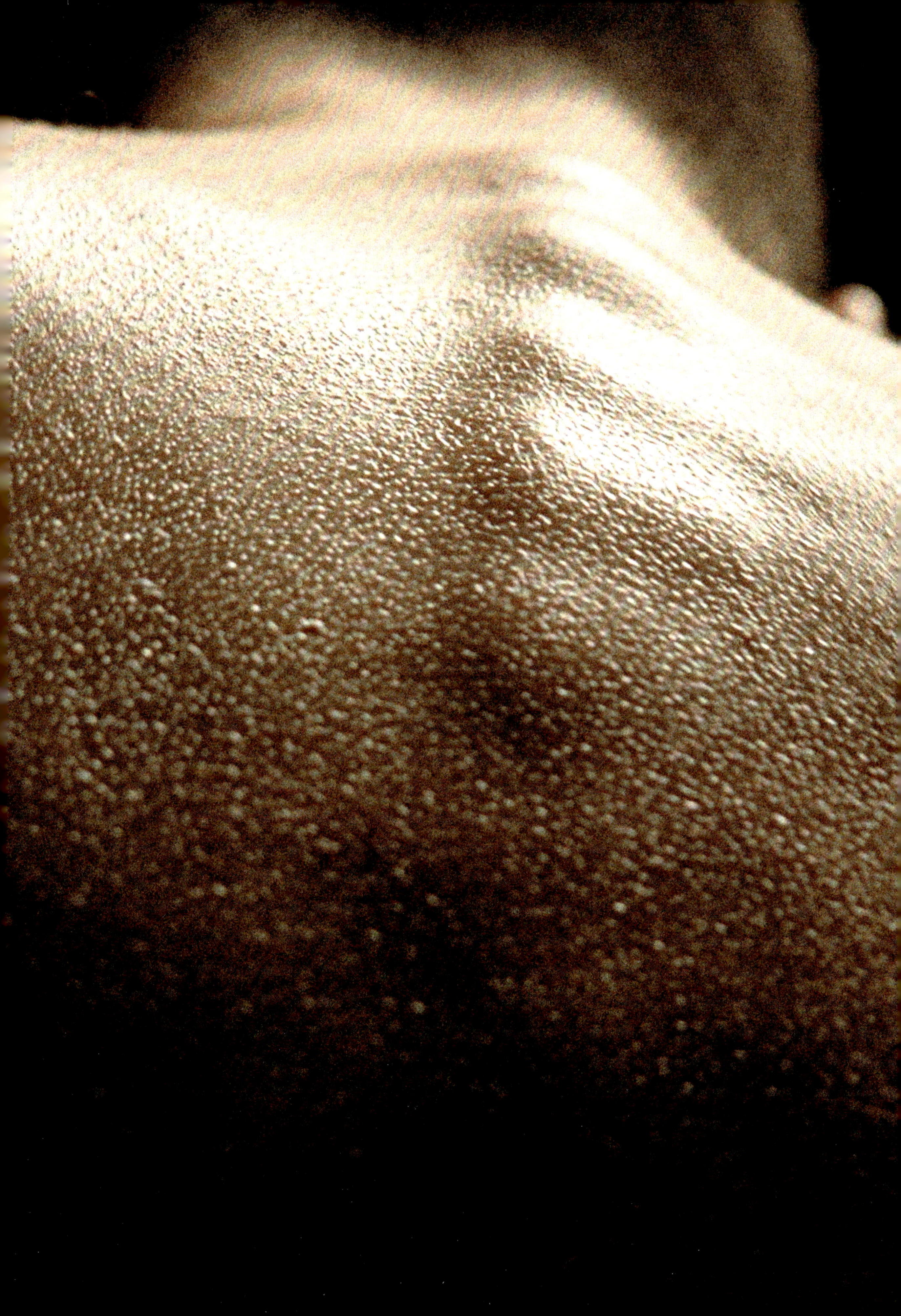

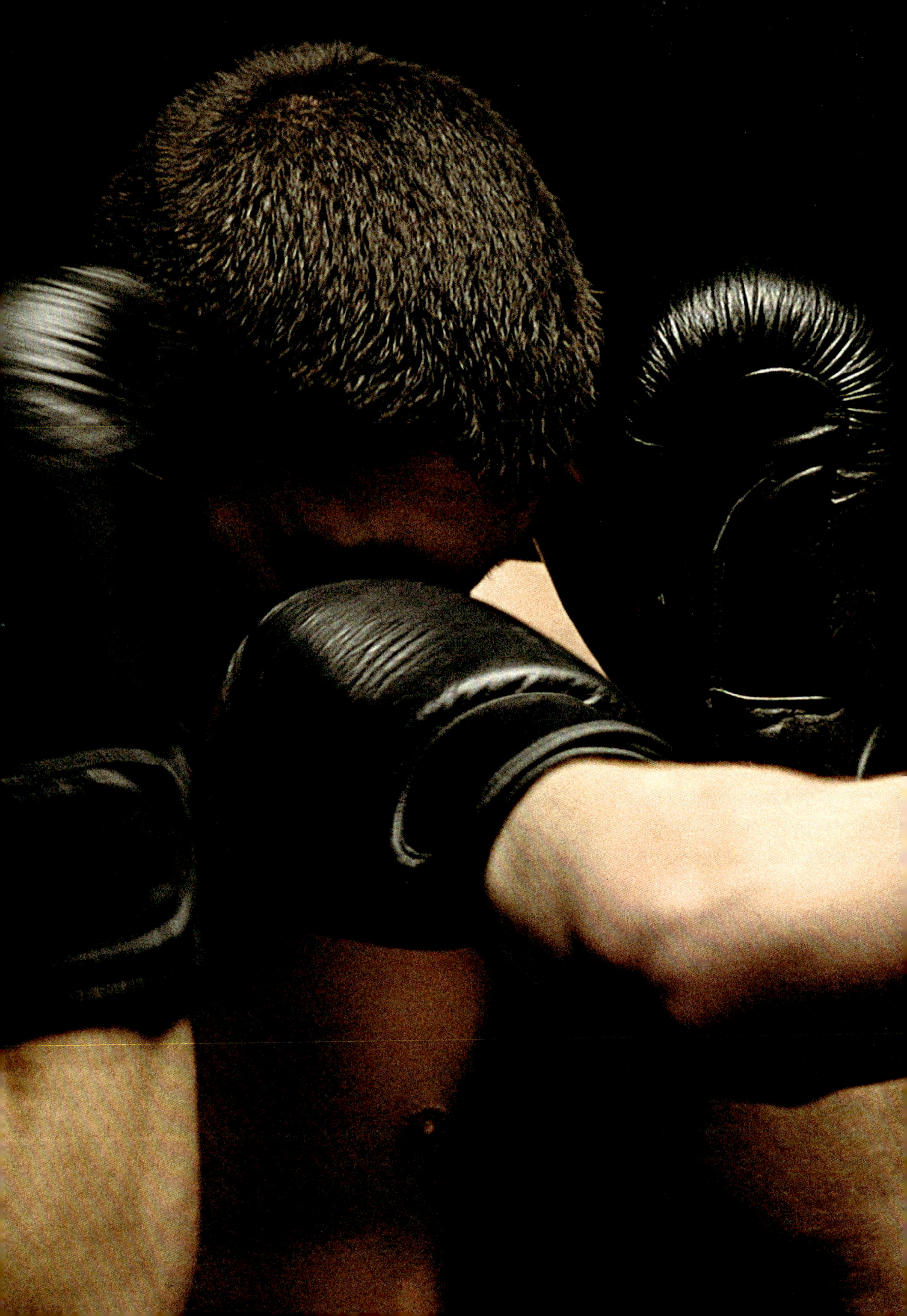

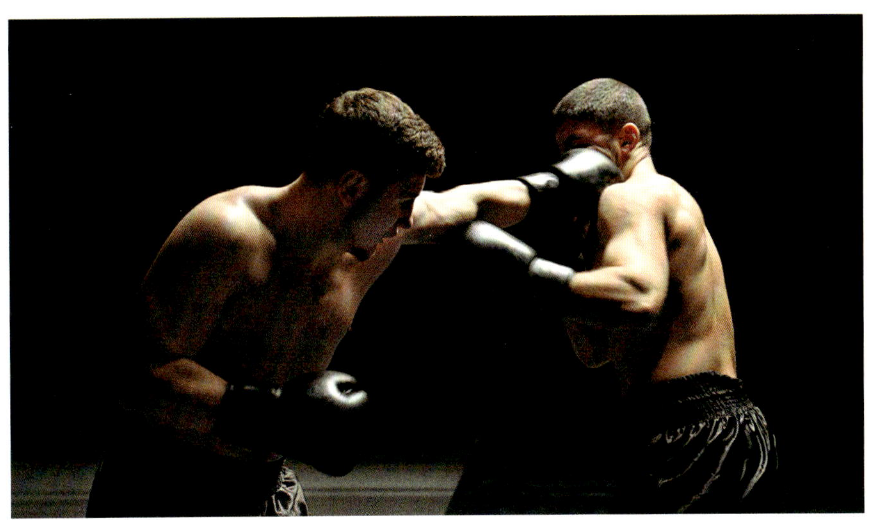

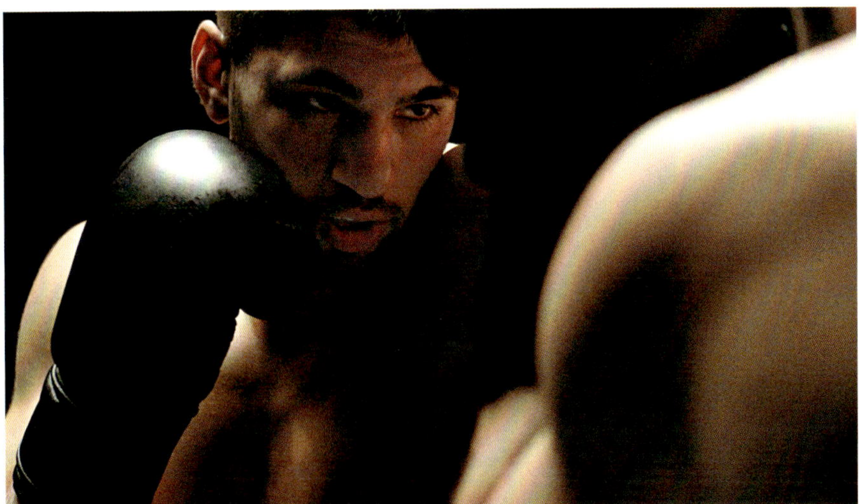

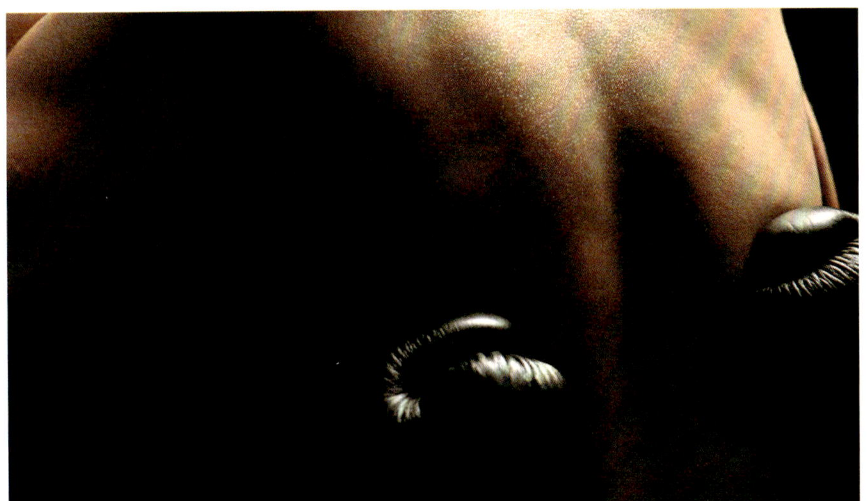

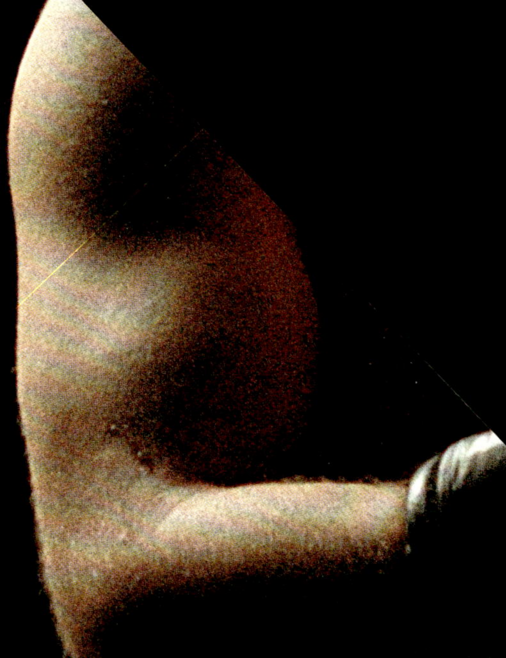

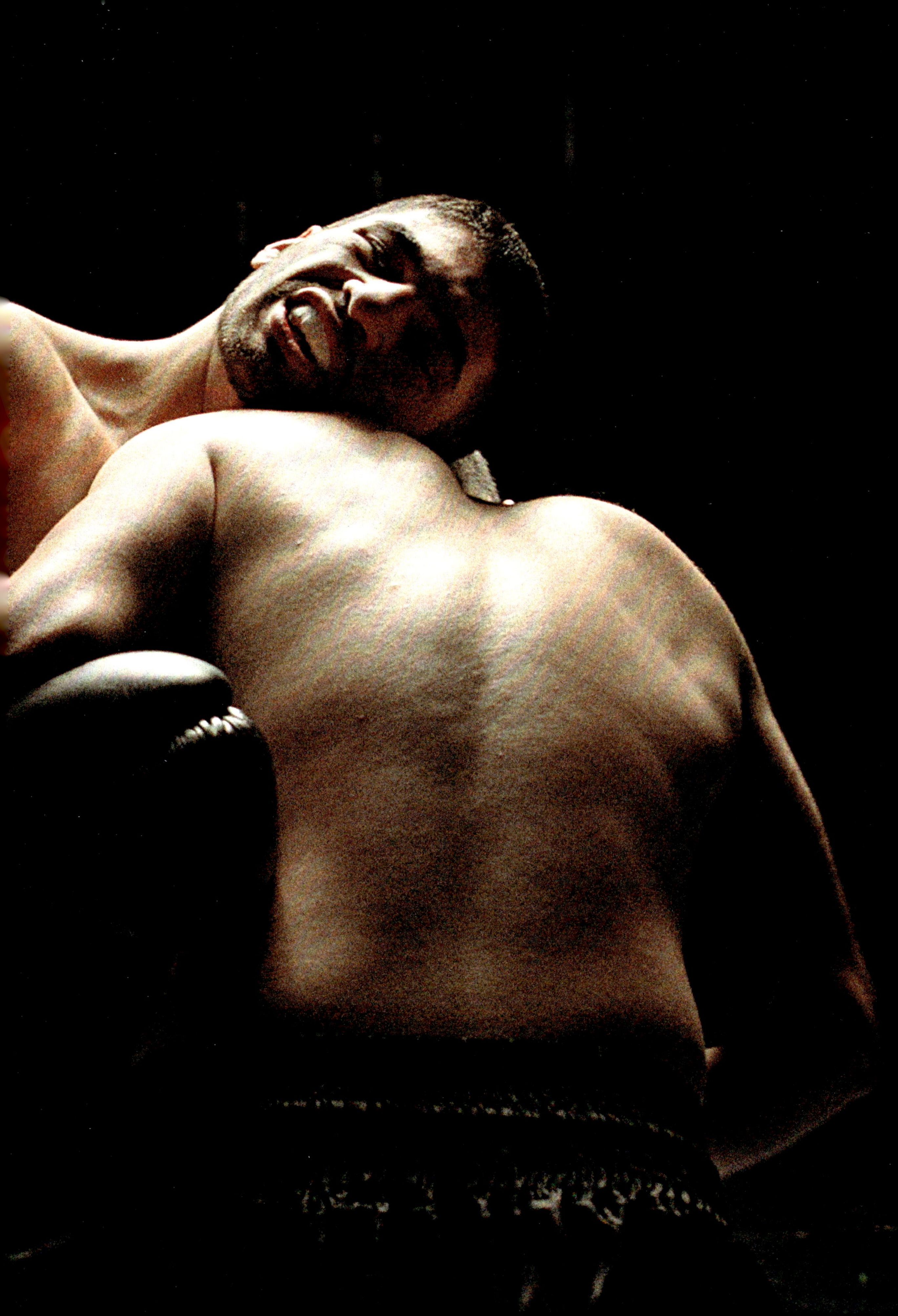

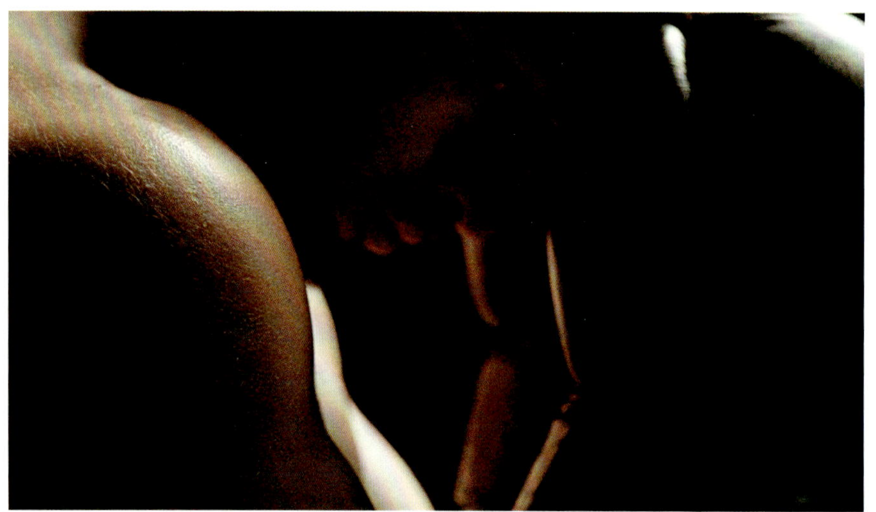
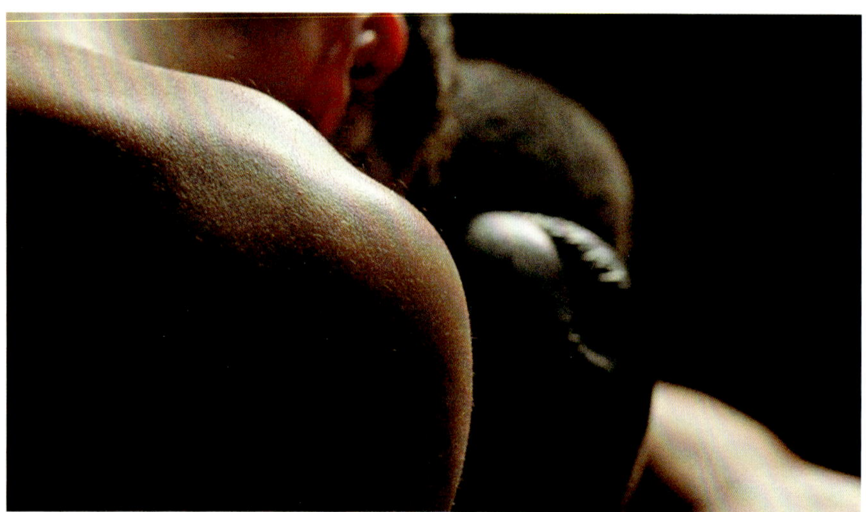
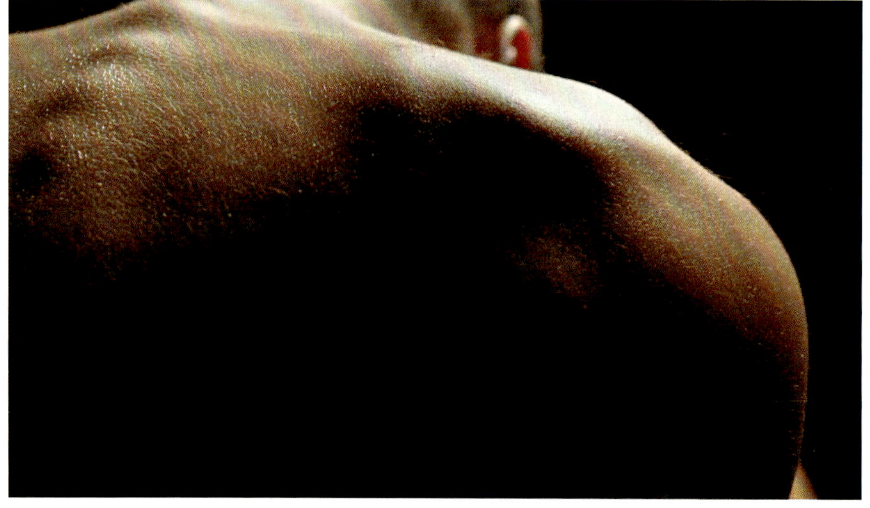

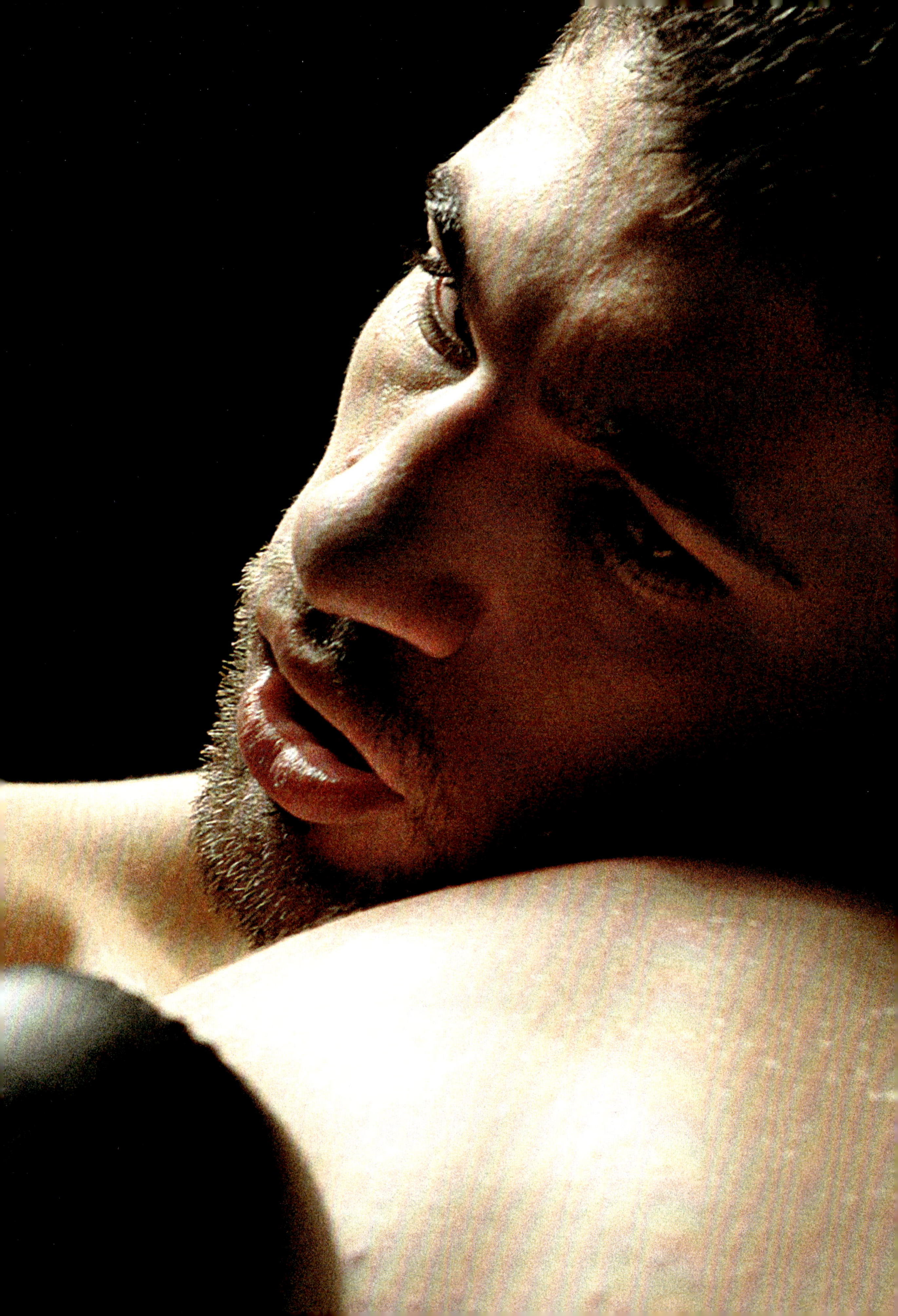

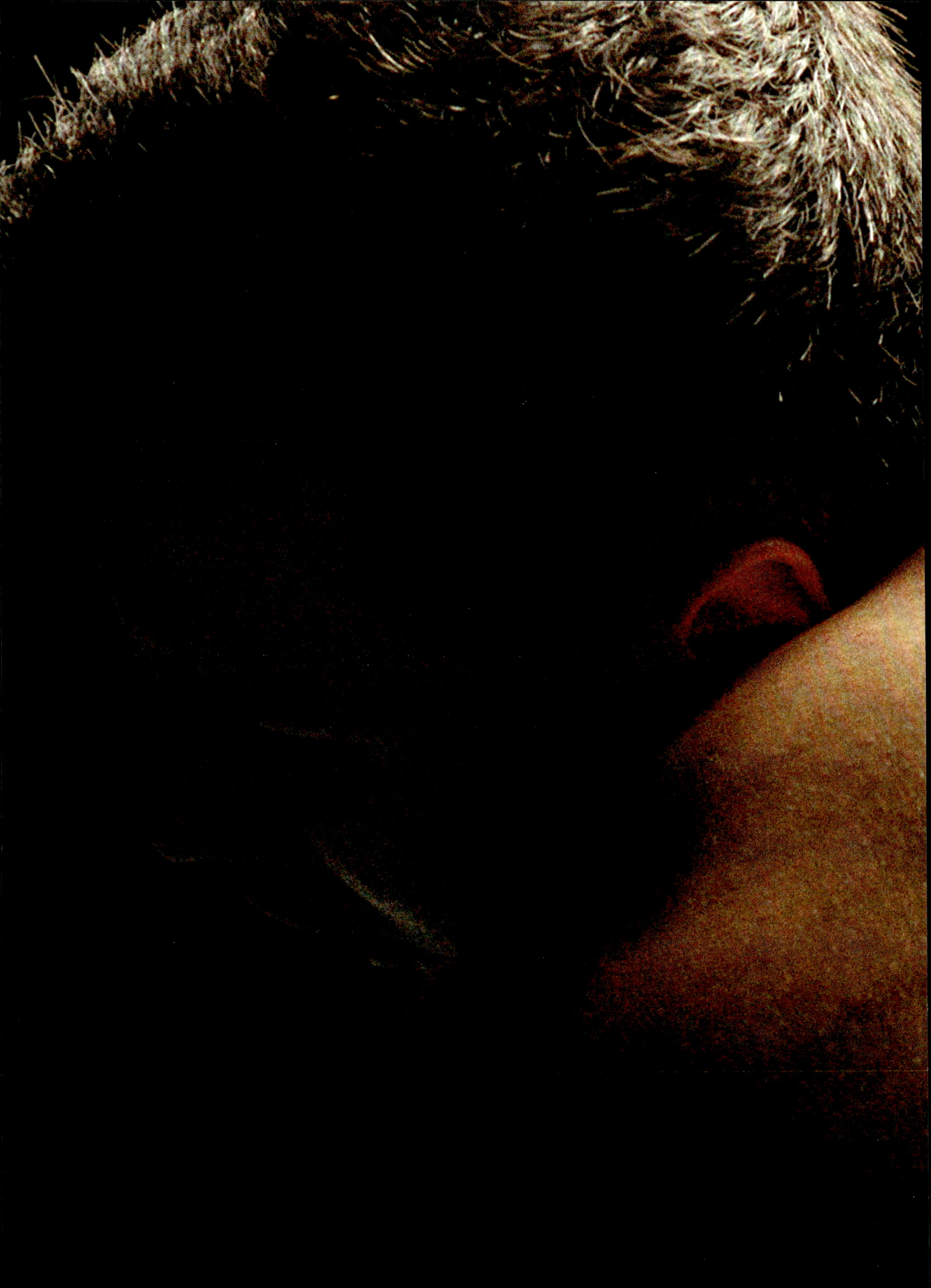

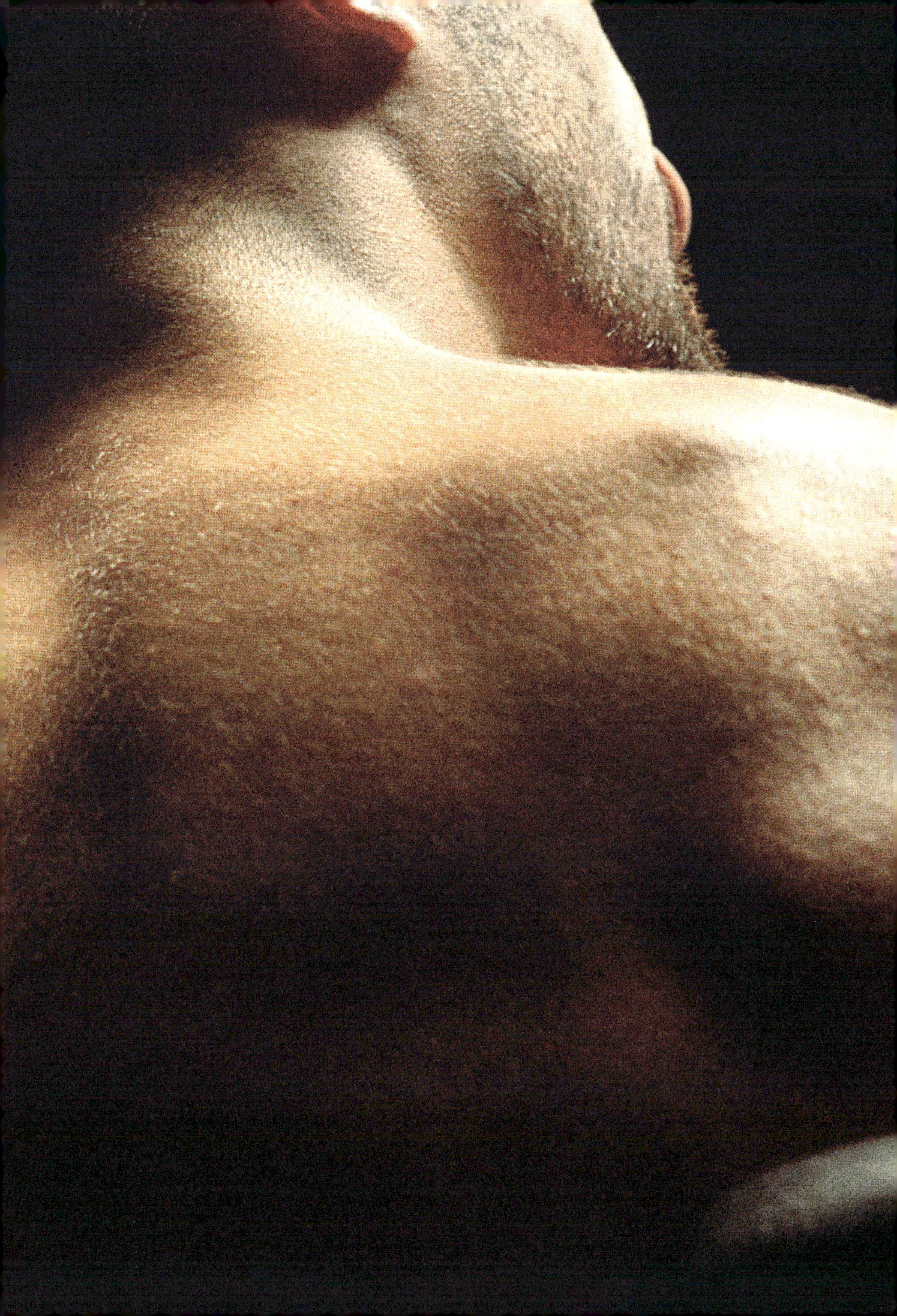

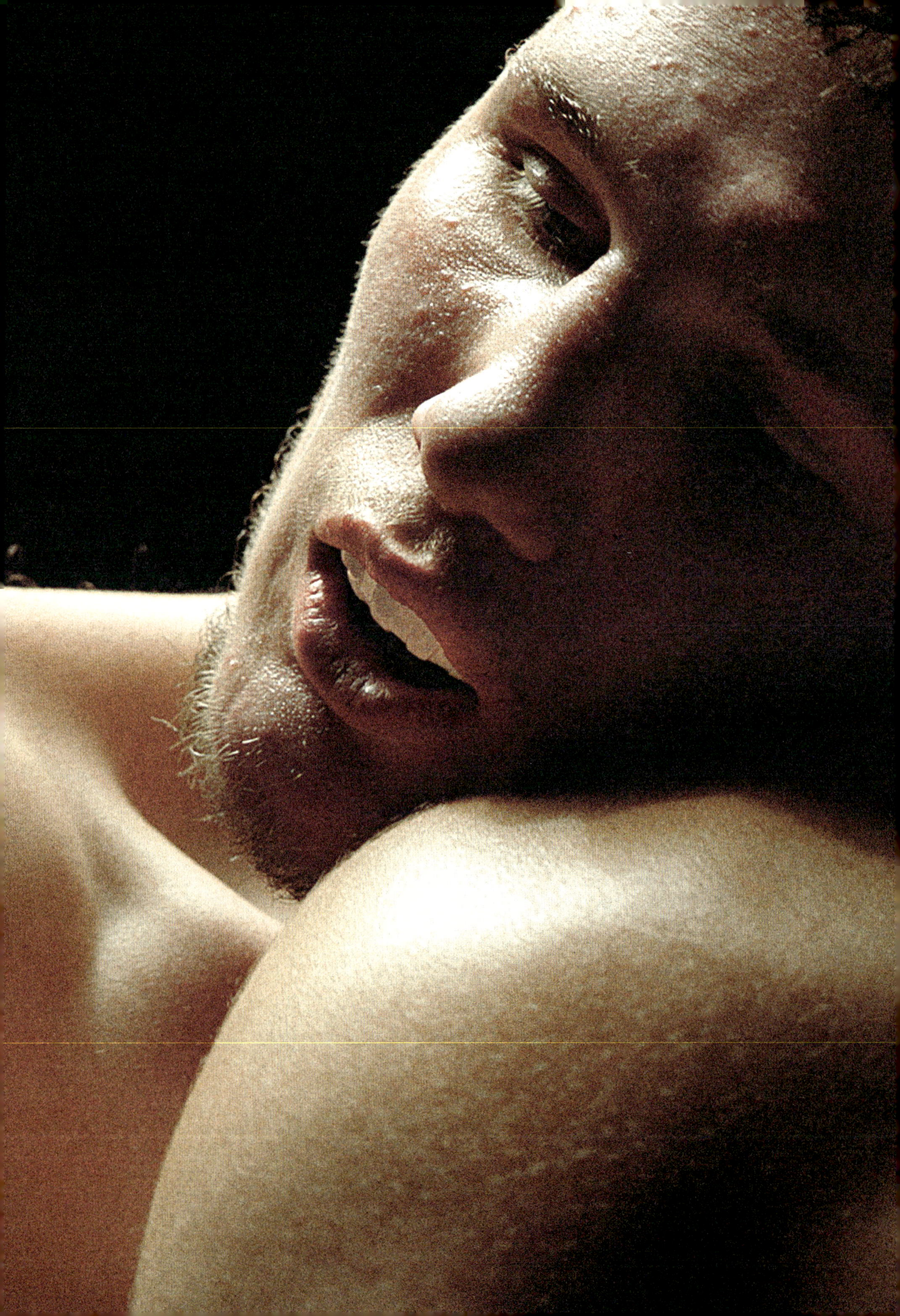

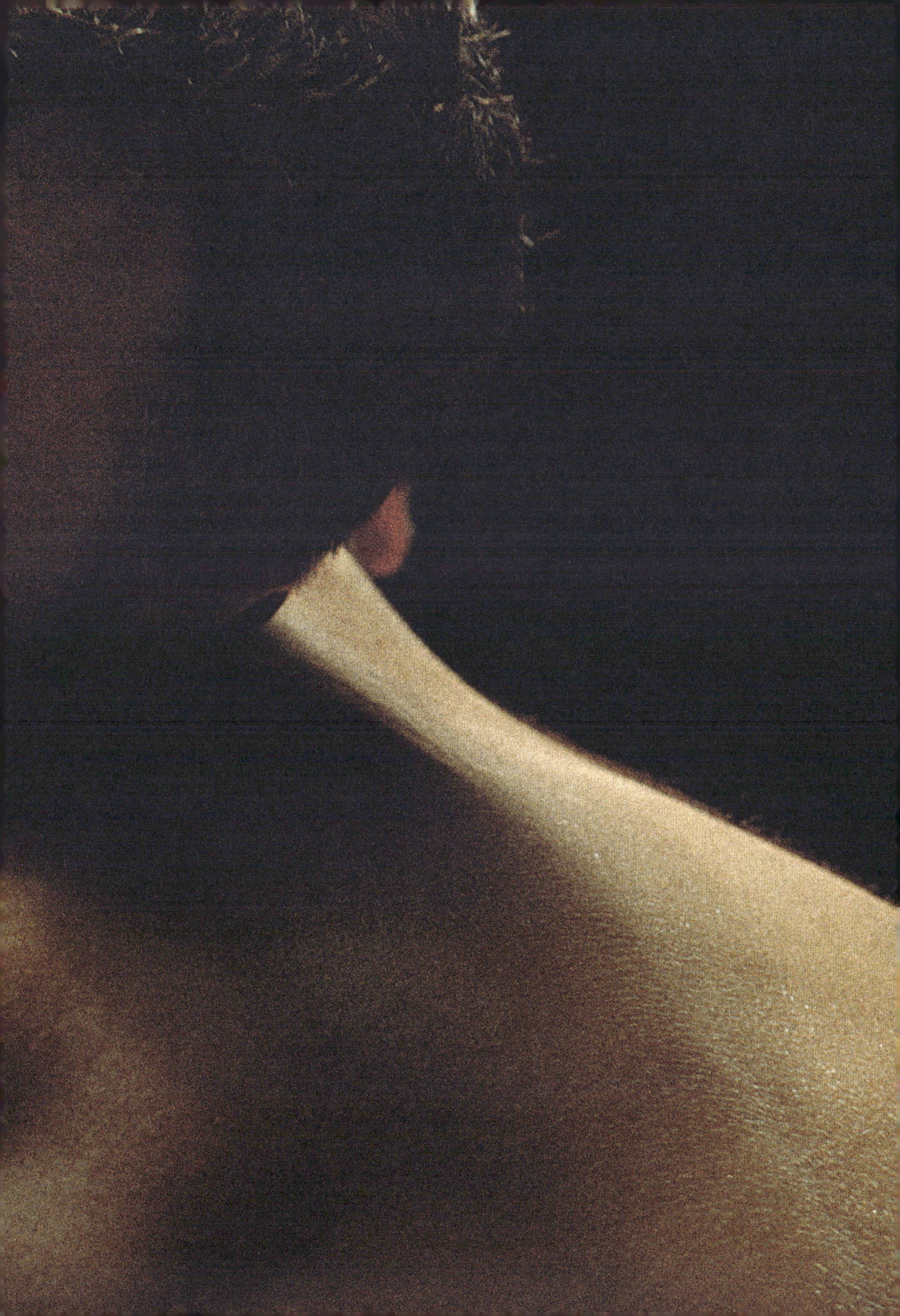

THE EPIC.
ASSOZIATIVES POTENZIAL VOR SCHWARZER KULISSE

MAURICE FUNKEN

THE EPIC: ASSOCIATIVE POTENTIAL IN FRONT OF A BLACK BACKDROP

MAURICE FUNKEN

»The most dominant male attributes [...] are aggression, a more actively focused sexuality, bonding with other men [...], the eroticization of male attributes [...] and the setting up of barriers between themselves and [...] men to retain a sense of individual male identity.« (Kim Gordon)[1]

Ein leises Knistern erinnert an eine Schallplatte, deren erste Töne noch nicht erklungen sind. Licht fällt auf eine aus der Dunkelheit des Raumes auftauchende unbewegte männliche Gestalt. Frontal im Blick ein markantes Gesicht, der freie Oberkörper trainiert, aber nicht übermäßig muskulös. Das Licht verlöscht. Eine weitere männliche Person von vergleichbarer Statur erscheint aus dem Schatten und tritt ins abermalig aufblendende Scheinwerferlicht. Das Licht verlöscht. Das Knistern bricht ab. Das Präludium ist zu Ende, die Protagonisten der Videoarbeit *The Epic* sind vorgestellt. Mit dem ersten Einsetzen einer sich langsam aufbauenden musikalischen Untermalung treten die beiden Boxer auf, treffen vor nicht näher definierter schwarzer Kulisse aufeinander. Pola Sieverding bedient sich hier des klassischen Chiaroscuros, setzt helle Figuren vor dunklen Raum.[2] Schon bald wechselt die Perspektive auf die beiden zunächst halbnah von der Seite gezeigten Männer. Eine gleitende Kamerafahrt beginnt, rotiert entlang der Begrenzungen eines imaginären Boxrings in einer 360-Grad-Bewegung um die Akteure. Die gesamte Videoarbeit wurde mit 200 Bildern pro Sekunde gedreht, wird jedoch in achtfacher Verlangsamung abgespielt.[3] Das Umkreisen wird so zu einem präzisen Untersuchen, einem detaillierten Aufzeichnen der Körper und dadurch zu einer offenen Reflexion über Körperbilder und Männlichkeit. Die Boxer verharren währenddessen in Bewegungslosigkeit. Das stetige Umfahren der Kamera wirkt geradezu diagnostisch, wie ein Scan, der eine Erfahrung der Figuren im Raum möglich macht.[4] Kann man Sieverdings Video der Boxer hiermit als eine in der Bewegung erstarrte Skulpturengruppe denken? Bernd und Hilla Bechers Fotografie ist als Skulptur verstanden worden, wieso dann nicht auch Video?[5] Eine Skulptur ist von allen Seiten erfahrbar, kann umrundet und aus verschiedenen Blickwinkeln betrachtet werden. Einzig der Mangel an Haptik lässt *The Epic* einer Plastik gegenüber zurücktreten.

Dieses Defizit versucht die Arbeit mit visuellen, aber auch akustischen Mitteln auszugleichen. Masse, Muskeln, Haare, Schweiß, Anstrengung und Schmerz – die

"The most dominant male attributes [...] are aggression, a more actively focused sexuality, bonding with other men [...], the eroticization of male attributes [...] and the setting up of barriers between themselves and [...] men to retain a sense of individual male identity." (Kim Gordon)[1]

Soft crackling sounds call to mind a record before its first tones play. Light falls on an unmoving male form surfacing out of the darkness of the space.There is a frontal view of a striking face, a bare chest, athletic but not excessively muscular. The light goes out. Another male person of comparable stature appears from the shadows and walks into a spotlight that is again turned on. The light goes out. The crackling sounds stop. The prelude has ended; the protagonists of the video work *The Epic* have been introduced. A slowly mounting musical backdrop begins as the two boxers enter, encountering one another in front of an undefined black background. Here Pola Sieverding makes use of classic chiaroscuro, placing brightly lit figures in front of a dark space.[2] Soon the perspective changes to show the two men, initially seen from the side in a medium shot. The camera begins to glide, rotating along the boundaries of an imaginary boxing ring, moving 360 degrees around the actors. The video work, filmed at 200 frames per second, is shown slowed down by a factor of eight.[3] The circling thus becomes a precise investigation, a detailed recording of bodies and an open reflection on images of bodies and masculinity. The boxers persist in their motionlessness. The continuous circumscribing with the camera has an almost diagnostic effect, like a scan making it possible to experience the figures in space.[4] Can Sieverding's video of boxers then be conceived as a sculptural group frozen in movement? If Bernd and Hilla Becher's photographs have been understood as sculpture, why not video too?[5] A sculpture can be experienced from all sides, can be walked around and observed from different points of view. All that *The Epic* lacks in comparison to a sculpture is the absence of the sense of touch.

The work seeks to compensate for this deficit both visually and acoustically. Body mass, muscles, hair, sweat, exertion and pain: the work focuses on the actors' physicality. When the actual boxing match begins, the bodies start to move. The sculptural moment that we have just described is left behind, even if the film, through its ongoing slow motion and the slowness of certain

Körperlichkeit der Akteure steht im Fokus der Arbeit. Sobald der eigentliche Boxkampf beginnt, geraten die Körper in Bewegung. Der soeben beschriebene skulpturale Moment ist aufgebrochen, auch wenn sich der Film angesichts der durchgängigen technischen Verlangsamung und der Langsamkeit mancher Handlungen der agierenden Personen diesem Augenblick immer wieder anzunähern vermag. Formal gesehen erzählt die Videoarbeit dabei eine geradlinige, lineare Narration. Der Betrachter verfolgt den sich entfaltenden Kampf Schlag um Schlag. Lange Einstellungen geben dem Geschehen Zeit, sich zu entfalten, während einzelne ausgewählte Momente des Zweikampfes von Sieverding hervorgehoben werden. Einen Schlag ins Leere zeigt sie etwa in Nahaufnahme. Auch setzt sie gezielt musikalische Akzente, tonale Versatzstücke einer fiebrigen, elektronischen Melodie, sobald die Intensität des Geschehens zunimmt, oftmals dicht gefolgt vom schweren Atem der erschöpften Boxer. Die Künstlerin hat den Film zum Teil parallel mit weiteren Geräuschen unterlegt, die zusammen mit der Musik eine akustische Ebene der Nähe und Intimität über die Bilder hinaus herstellen. Die Leere des Ortes als statisches Rauschen, die Schritte, den Atem und den Herzschlag der Boxer collagiert sie nuanciert zu einem den Film untermalenden Soundscape. Dabei entwickeln gerade die Geräusche ein assoziatives Potenzial, das sich vor allem dann entfaltet, wenn etwas nicht eindeutig im Blick der Kamera liegt oder gar *off-screen* passiert, etwa ein Schlag nicht sichtbar, aber hörbar seinen Gegner findet. In dem tief-dumpfen Nachhall wird der Schlag in seiner vollen Wucht und Kraft für den Betrachter deutlich physisch spürbar und präsent.

Geradezu haptisch erfahrbar wird darüber hinaus auf der visuellen Ebene die Körperlichkeit der beiden Männer, je weiter das Kampfgeschehen voranschreitet. Nasser Schweiß glänzt im hellen Scheinwerferlicht auf den dem Betrachter zugewandten Rücken der Boxer in Nahaufnahme vor schwarzem Hintergrund. Die an Helldunkelmalerei erinnernde dramatische Ausleuchtung verstärkt die dreidimensionale Wirkung der Körper, der Schein des gleißenden Lichtes lässt die Haut der Akteure farbig schimmern. Sieverdings Bildsprache wird hier bedeutend sinnlicher, weniger beobachtend, die Kamera spielt mit Unschärfen und Schärfen, Haare oder gar Hautporen sind sichtbar. Wenn ein Schlag in Zeitlupe einen der beiden Sportler trifft, werden die Kräfte sichtbar, die

movements of the actors, repeatedly re-approaches this moment. The video relates a linear narration from a formal perspective. The viewer follows the fight blow by blow as it progresses. Long takes give the events time to unfold, while Sieverding emphasizes selected moments of the duel. A punch that misses its mark, for example, she shows in close-up. She also makes targeted use of music for emphasis, the tonal scenery of a fevered electronic melody heard as the intensity of the action increases, often followed by the exhausted boxers' heavy breathing. In parallel, the artist adds certain other sounds that, alongside the music, produce an acoustical level of closeness and intimacy beyond the images. She makes a collage of nuances of the recorded static heard in the absence of sound, sound's "empty space," the footfalls, the breathing and the boxers' heartbeats into a soundscape that serves as a background for the film. The sounds develop an associative potential of their own, especially expressed when something is not clear in the camera's gaze or happens off-screen, for example when a punch is landed on an opponent, not visibly, but audibly. In the deep muffled echoes, the blow becomes unmistakably tangible and present for the spectator in all its impact and force.

The two men's physicality becomes almost palpable on the visual plane as the fight goes on. Moist sweat shines on the boxers' backs, turned to the audience and brightly lit by a spotlight, in close-up on a black background. The dramatic lighting, reminiscent of chiaroscuro painting, intensifies the bodies' three-dimensional effect. The glittering light causes the actors' skin to shimmer with colors. Sieverding's visual language grows significantly more sensual, less observational. The camera plays with blur and focus. Hair, even pores are visible. When one of the two athletes is punched in slow motion, it is possible to see the physical forces colliding and rippling through the bodies. Flesh and form oscillate; physicality is made discernible.

The final act is the two fighters' clinch, which is defining for the work's narrative. Here the film develops an ambiguous associative potential, at first on a purely visual level. It is a sensual moment of athletic rivalry and physical proximity, a mixture of capitulation and exhaustion, tension and release, a last rearing up, a last blow. Aggression encounters and opposes sympathy. Boundaries blur and are transgressed. Everything is open and possible when distance falls away. Sieverding

auf die Körper einwirken. Fleisch und Form geraten in Schwingung, Körperlichkeit wird erkennbar.

Im finalen, die Narrative der Arbeit bestimmenden Akt des Clinches der beiden Kämpfer entwickelt der Film ein mehrdeutiges assoziatives Potenzial zunächst auf rein visueller Ebene. Es ist ein sinnlicher Moment von sportlicher Rivalität und körperlicher Nähe, eine Mischung aus Kapitulation und Erschöpfung, Spannung und Entspannung, ein letztes Aufbäumen, ein letzter Schlag. Aggression trifft auf und arbeitet gegen Zuneigung. Grenzen verwischen und werden überschritten, alles ist offen, alles ist möglich, wenn die Distanz fehlt. Sieverding vermag damit subtil wie bereits in früheren fotografischen Arbeiten zugewiesene und potenziell gesetzte Rollen von Männlichkeit und Körpercodes zu hinterfragen. Der Clinch als Augenblick der Annäherung zweier schwitzender, halbnackter Männer ist bewusst uneindeutig und denkbar homoerotisch konnotiert.[6] Die schwarze Leere des Raums gibt der zärtlich-aggressiven Spannung die nötige Intimität, schafft es, Geschlechterrollen auszusetzen und die wahre Identität freizulegen. Maskulin erlerntes Verhalten pausiert in diesem zeitlos-sinnlichen Nexus und steht zur Disposition. Der Clinch wird damit zu einem nonverbalen Diskurs über Männlichkeit. Männliche Aggression, Sexualität, Bonding, Erotisierung, Grenzen und Identität stehen im Zentrum des Clinches, dem Sieverding endlos viel Zeit gibt, sich zu entfalten, und der gerade in der Verlangsamung an Schönheit und Kraft gewinnt. Mehr Gewicht verleiht der Szene eine bereits bekannte akustische Untermalung, die sich als Variation des ersten musikalischen Themas der Videoarbeit herausstellt. Damit spannt Sieverding einen Bogen zum Beginn des Films.[7] Auch narrativ schließt das Ende zum Ausgangspunkt von *The Epic* an, lösen sich doch die Boxer aus dem Moment des Clinches. Nicht ohne einen abschließenden Blick auf den anderen zu werfen, gehen die beiden Sportler vor schwarzer Kulisse auseinander. Das Ende ist offen, es wird weder Sieger noch Verlierer benannt. Ein erneutes Zusammentreffen ist stets möglich und wahrscheinlich: Die Arbeit wird im Loop gezeigt.

is able to subtly question assigned and potentially settled roles of masculinity and body codes, as she has done in her earlier photographic works already. The clinch as a moment of closeness for two sweating, half-naked men is, in connotation, consciously unclear and conceivably homoerotic.[6] The black emptiness of the space endows the tender yet aggressive tension with the necessary intimacy, succeeding in suspending gender roles and exposing real identity. Masculine behavior or rather behavior that has been learned as masculine is paused in this timeless sensual nexus and thrown open to question. The clinch thus becomes a non-verbal discourse on masculinity. Male aggression, sexuality, bonding, eroticization, boundaries and identity are at the center of the clinch which Sieverding gives an infinity of time to develop, gaining beauty and power precisely because it is slowed down. The scene takes on greater weight through its acoustical underpinnings, which prove to be a variation of the video work's first musical theme. Thus Sieverding closes the circle and returns to the film's beginning.[7] Narratively, too, *The Epic's* ending links back to its point of departure. The boxers depart from the moment of the clinch. The two athletes take leave of one another, not without casting a parting look at one another. The ending is open, naming neither winners nor losers. Another meeting is always possible and probable: the work is shown in a loop.

1 Kim Gordon, »Unresolved Desires«, in: Branden W. Joseph (Hrsg.), *Kim Gordon. Is It My Body? Selected Texts*, New York 2014, S. 63 f.

2 In der Fotoserie *Arena* verfuhr sie ähnlich. Auch dort wurde ein mögliches Publikum konsequent ausgeschwärzt, sodass der Betrachter mit den Protagonisten des Films allein ist.

3 Dass die gesamte Laufzeit des Films damit rund 24 Minuten beträgt, ist kein Zufall. Pola Sieverding hat exakt drei Minuten Filmmaterial zusammengetragen, entsprechend der Dauer einer tatsächlichen Runde im Boxen.

4 In der Ausstellung der Arbeit hat auch der Betrachter die Möglichkeit zu einem solchen Umkreisen: Die Leinwand ist so im dunklen Raum platziert, dass sie von beiden Seiten sichtbar ist. Damit entspricht die Art der Präsentation formal der Idee der Arbeit. Zudem wird mit der in der Ausstellung platzierten Tribünenarchitektur ein konkreter Verweis auf den Schauplatz sportlicher Wettkämpfe und ihre historische Konnotation gegeben.

5 Bernd und Hilla Becher erhielten auf der Biennale in Venedig 1990 den Preis für Skulptur für ihre Fotoarbeiten zur anonymen Skulptur. Siehe Tobia Bezzola, »Von der Skulptur in der Fotografie zur Fotografie als Plastik«, in: Roxana Marcoci (Hrsg.), *FotoSkulptur. Die Fotografie der Skulptur 1839 bis heute*, Ostfildern-Ruit 2011, S. 28 ff.

6 Die Videoarbeit *Bear* von Steve McQueen aus dem Jahr 1993 experimentiert wie Sieverdings Werk mit mehrdeutigen Körperbildern und operiert darüber hinaus weitaus offener mit homoerotischen Deutungsmustern. Vgl. Susanne Gaensheimer, »Geschichten des Augenblicks«, in: Helmut Friedel (Hrsg.), *Geschichten des Augenblicks. Über Narration und Langsamkeit*, Ostfildern-Ruit 1999, S. 31 f.

7 Auch das bereits benannte schallplattenähnliche Knistern verweist auf die Möglichkeit des Neubeginns. Wie eine Schallplatte kann man Sieverdings Videoarbeit potenziell immer wieder abspielen, indem man die Nadel neu auf das Vinyl setzt.

1 Kim Gordon, "Unresolved Desires," in: Kim Gordon, *Is It My Body? Selected Texts*, ed. Branden W. Joseph (New York: Sternberg Press, 2014), p. 63f.

2 She took a similar approach with the photo series *Arena*, in which a potential audience was consistently blacked out as well, leaving the viewer alone with the film's protagonists.

3 It is no coincidence that the film's total running time is 24 minutes. Pola Sieverding gathered exactly three minutes of film material, matching the duration of an actual round of boxing.

4 The viewer has the opportunity to do this kind of circling when viewing the work at the exhibition. The screen is placed in a dark room in such a way as to be viewable from both sides. This creates a formal correspondence between the manner of presentation and the idea underlying the work. In addition, the architecture of raised seating at the exhibition makes a specific reference to the site of athletic competitions and their historical connotation.

5 Bernd and Hilla Becher were awarded the prize for sculpture at the 1990 Venice Biennale for their photographs of anonymous sculpture. See Tobia Bezzola, "From Sculpture in Photography to Photography as Plastic Art," in: Roxana Marcoci, ed., *The Original Copy: Photography of Sculpture, 1839 to Today* (New York: Museum of Modern Art, 2010), p. 28ff.

6 Like Sieverding's work, Steve McQueen's 1993 video *Bear* experiments with polyvalent body images. It also plays more freely with homoerotic interpretations. See Susanne Gaensheimer, "Moments in Time," in: Helmut Friedel, ed., *Moments in Time: On Narration and Slowness* (Ostfildern: Hatje Cantz, 1999), p. 31f.

7 The record-like crackling sound we have discussed also refers to the possibility of a new beginning. Sieverding's video work, like a record, has the potential to be played an infinite number of times by placing the needle back on the vinyl.

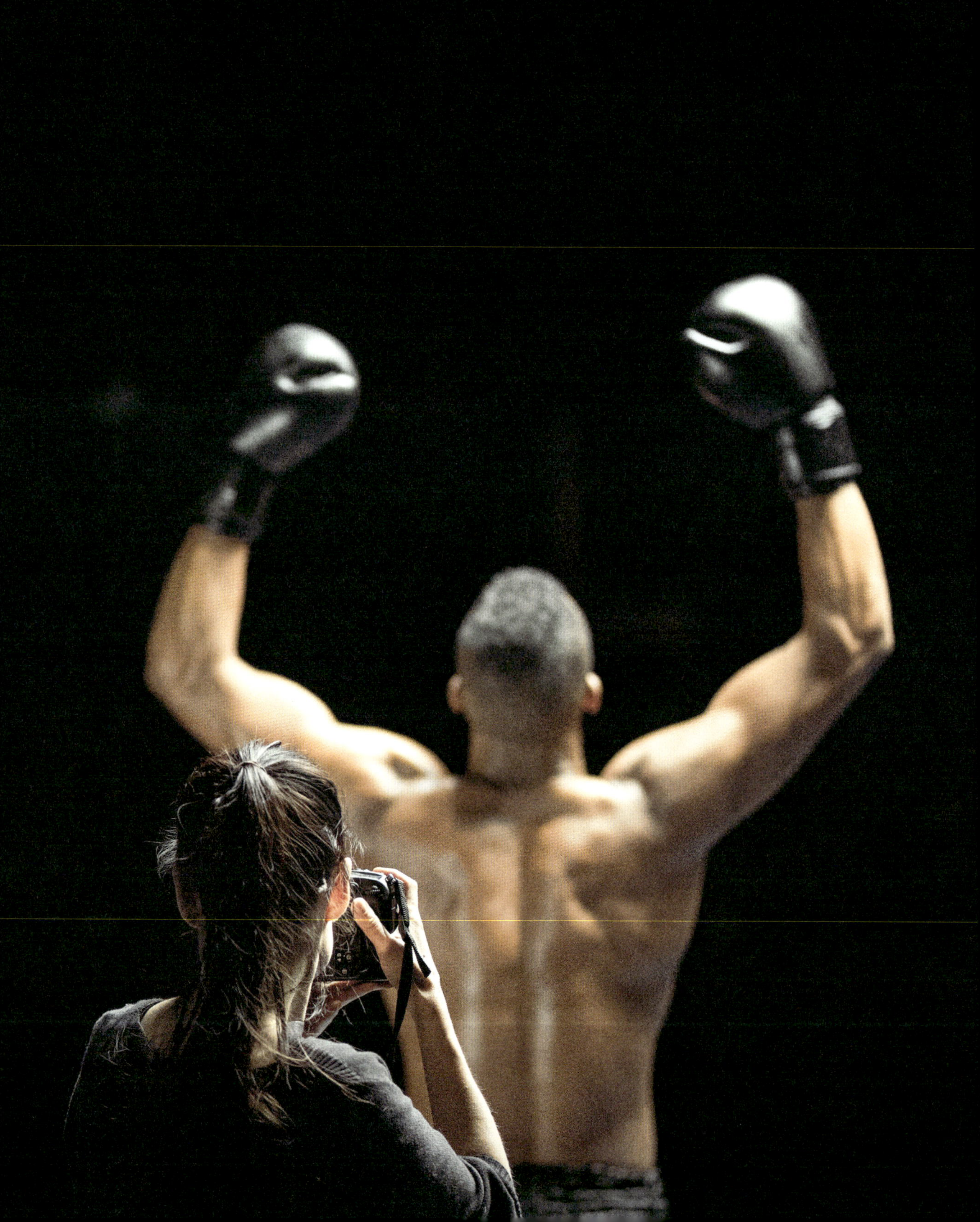

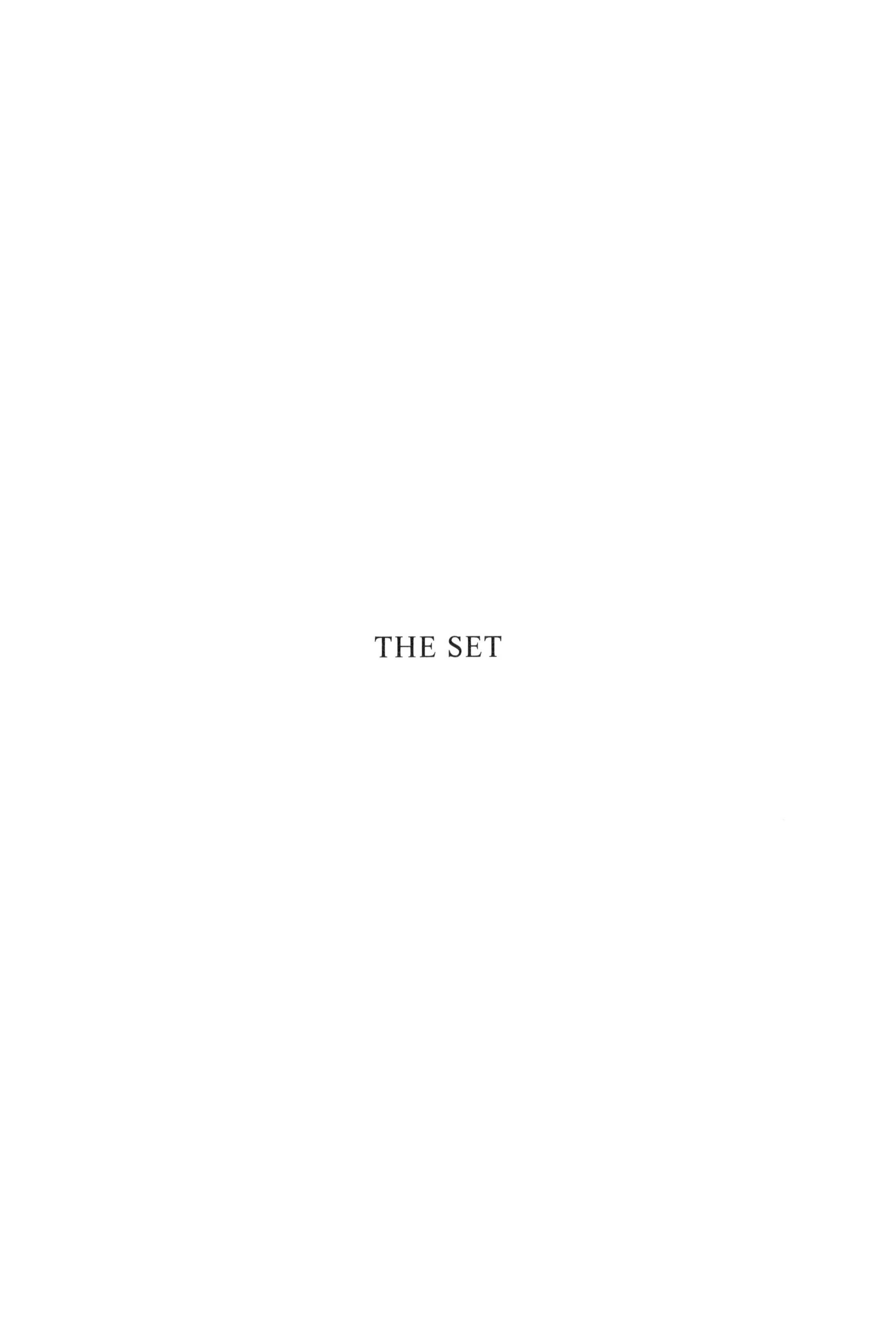

THE SET

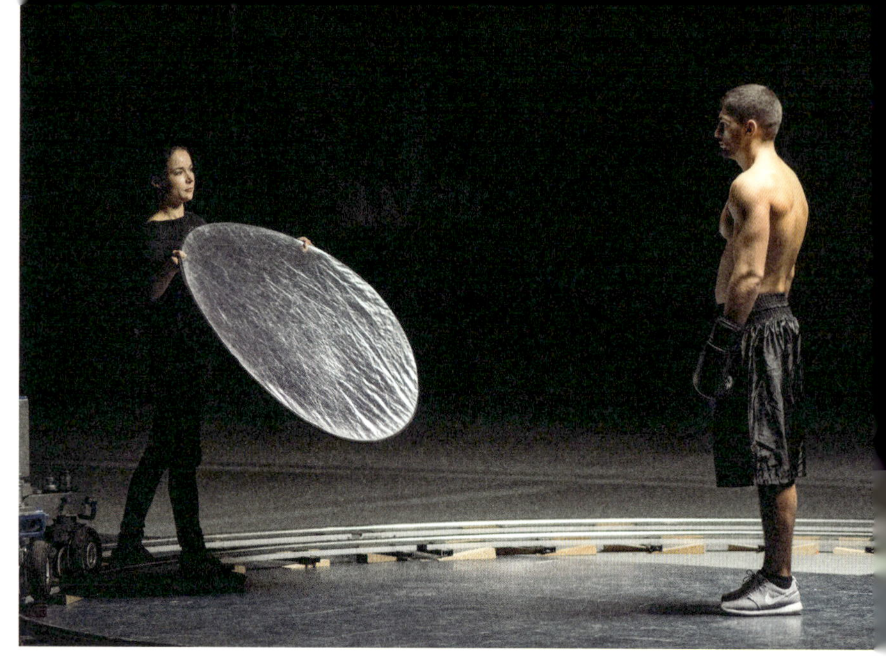

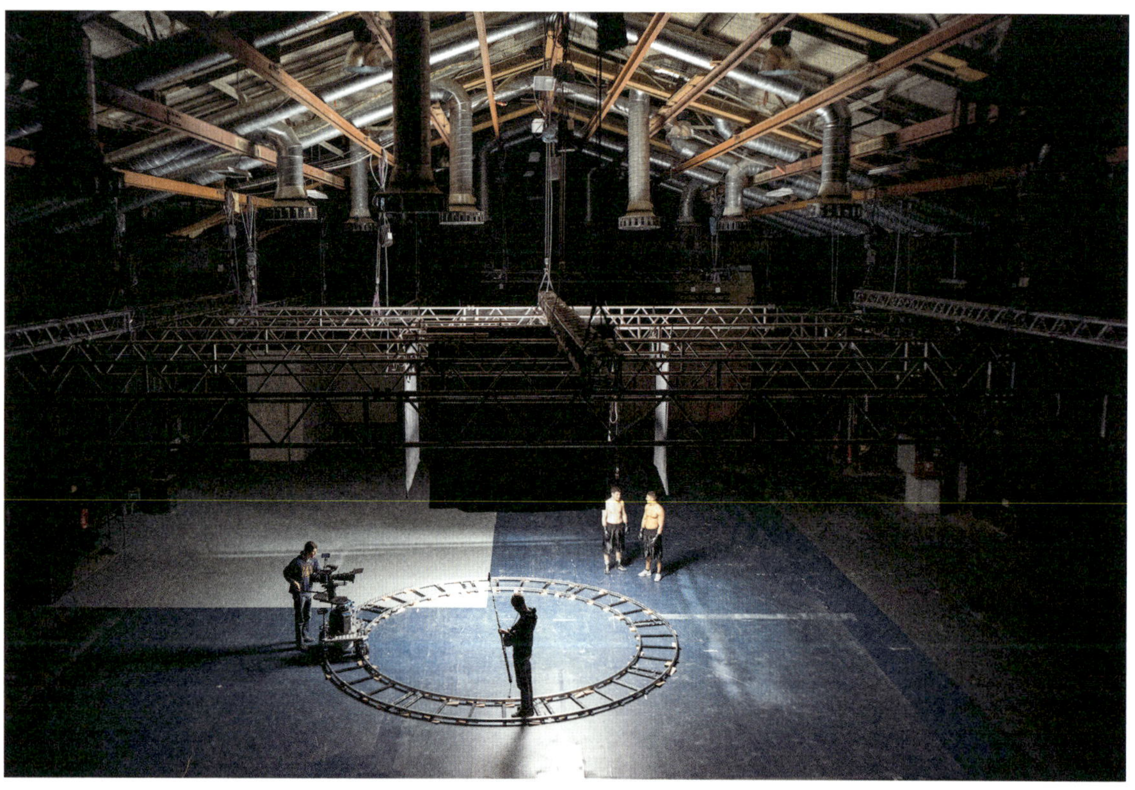

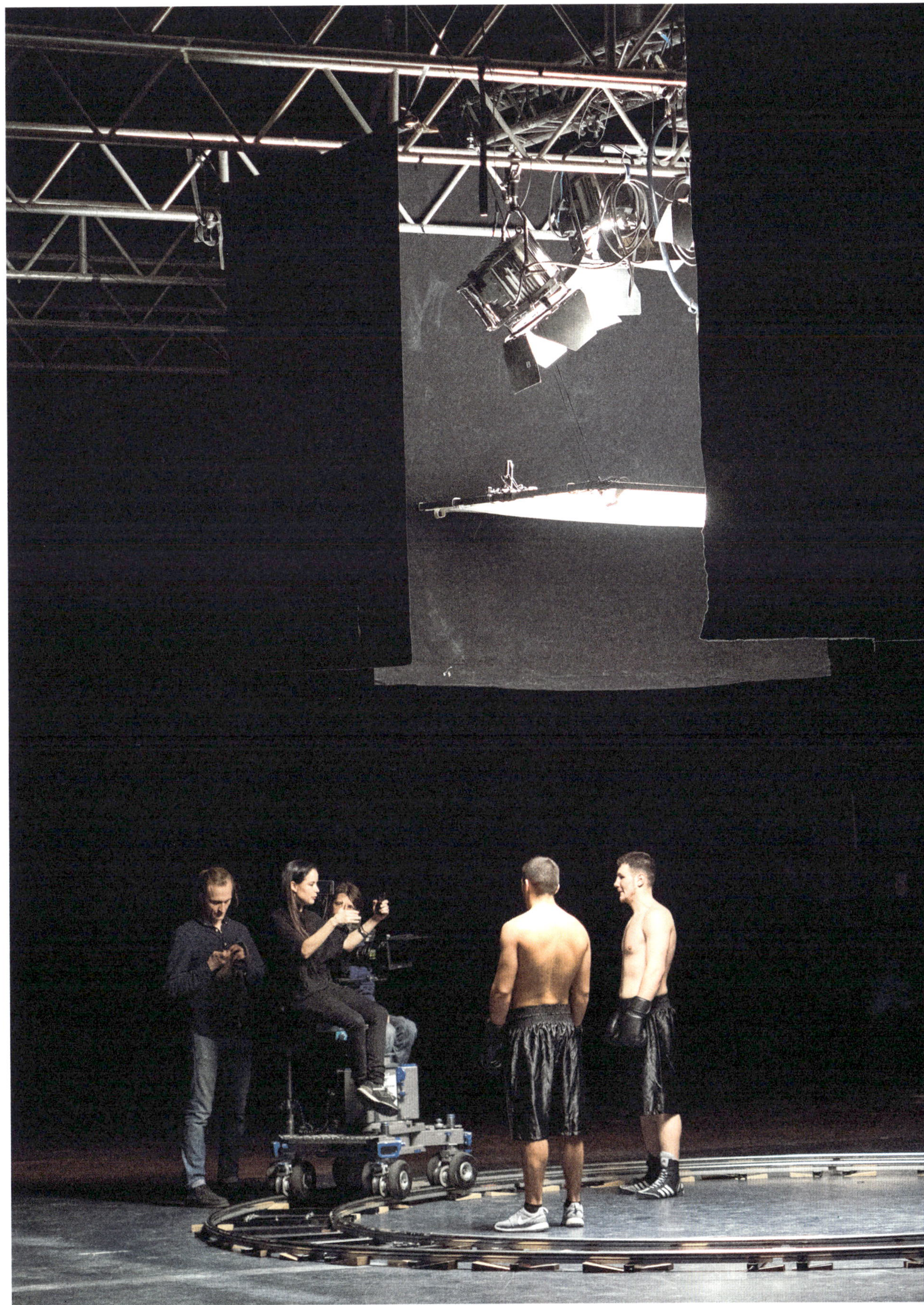

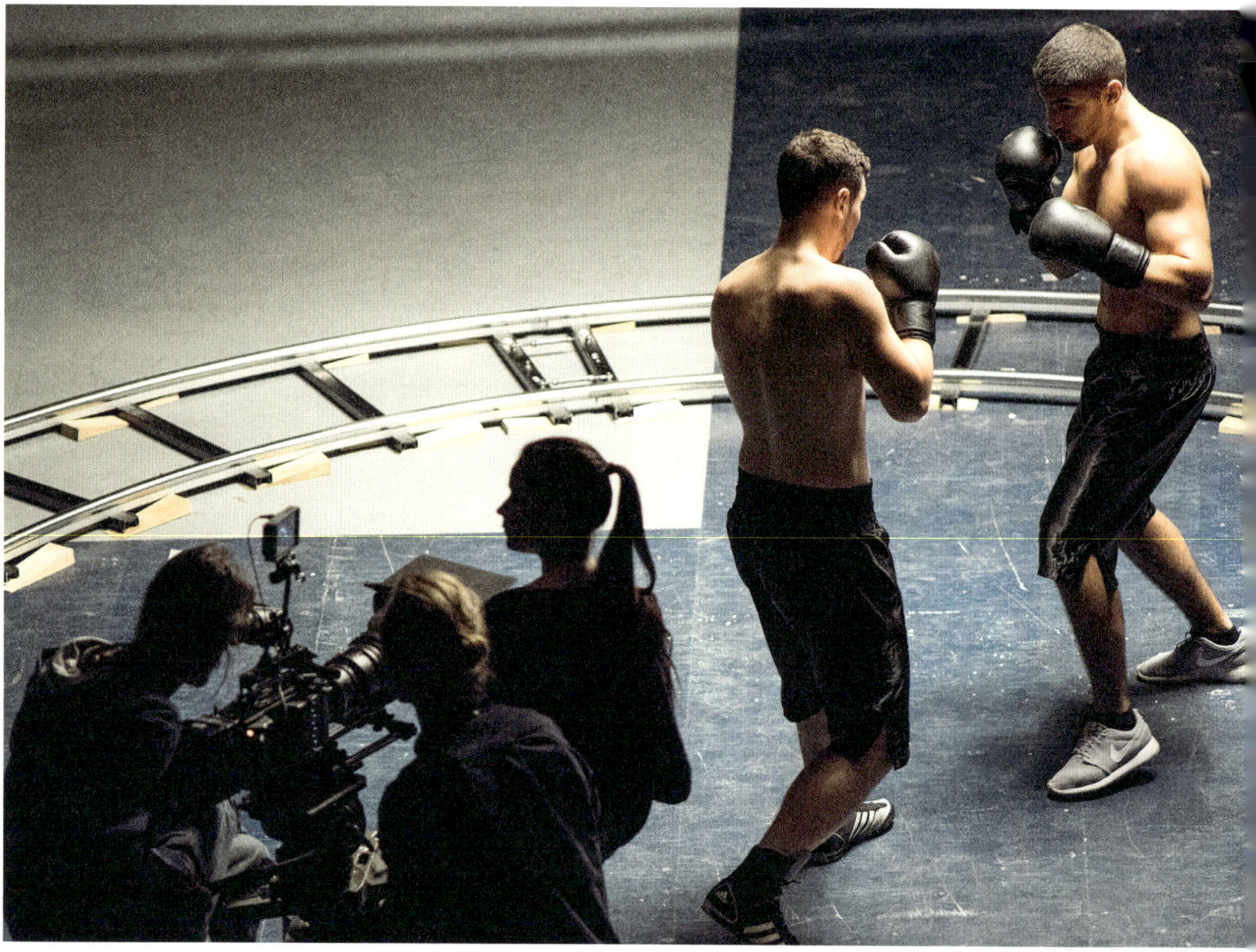

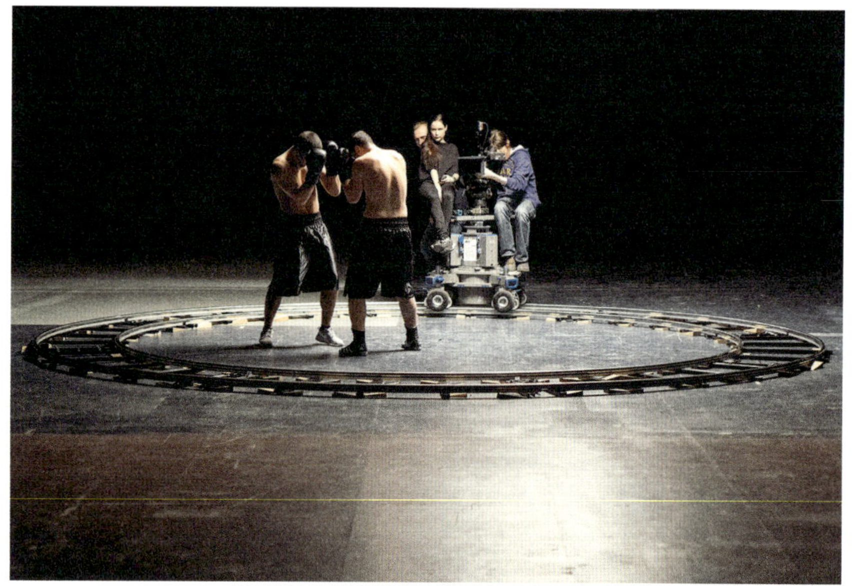

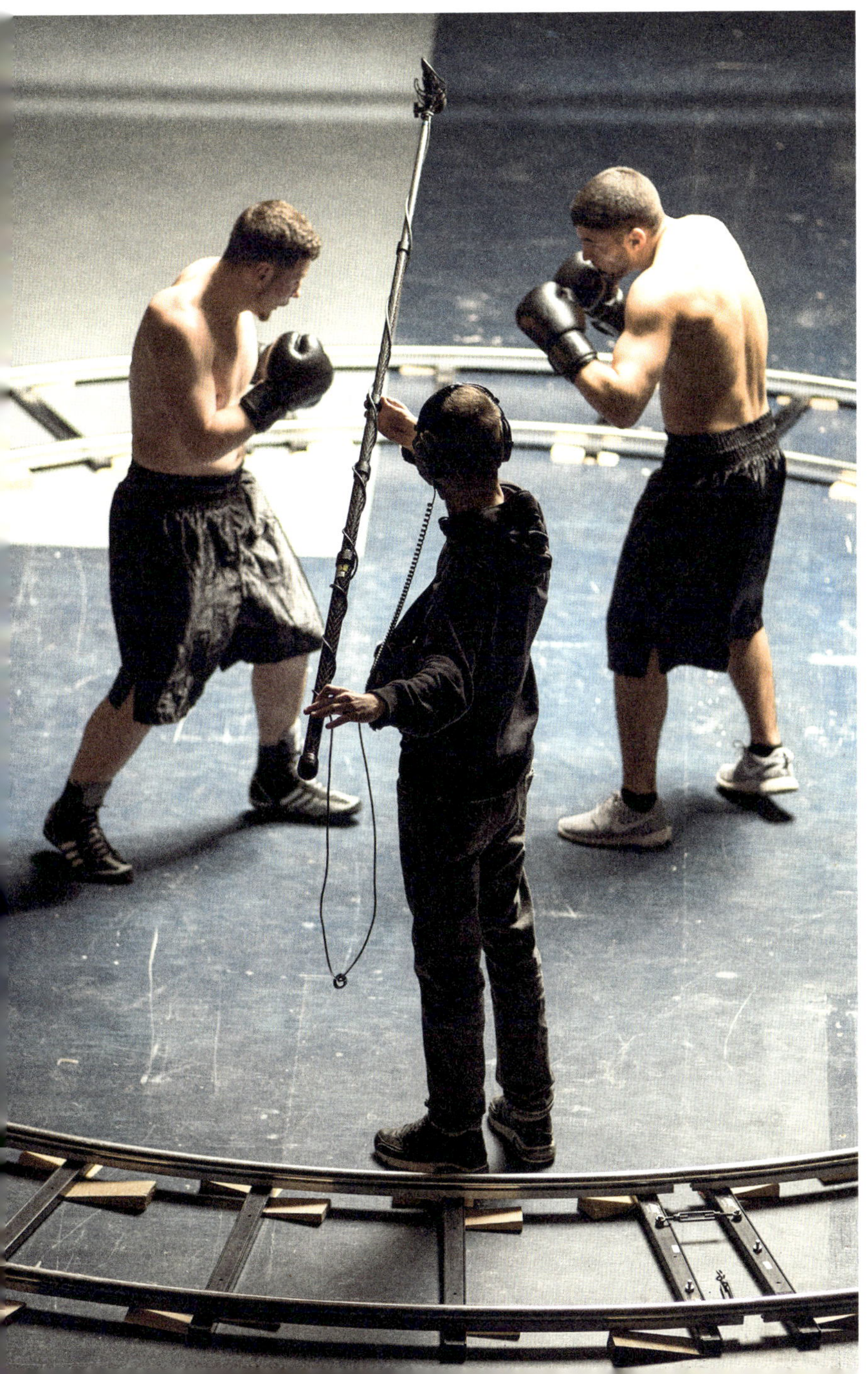

Pola Sieverding möchte sich bei folgenden Personen bedanken / Pola Sieverding would like to thank the following people:

Frank Bartsch
Pierre Becker
Christopher Berg
Oscar Betlejewski
Gideon Böhm
Johanna Buffetrille
Maurice Funken
Joëlle Grosz
GWF German Wrestling Federation
Friederike Hamann
Moritz Hirsch
Julian Holzapfel
Kay Huste
Dirk Käsebier
Abdullah Karalioglu
Ben Kaufmann
Ilja Kloppenburg
Barbara Könches
Thomas Koester
Michael Kohtes
Robert Krug
Benjamin Letzler
Holger Liebs
LINK
Anna Jill Lüpertz
Kirsten Maar
Azamat Machmudov
Christoph Manz
MAP Markus Ambach Projekte
Klaus Mettig
Alena Julie Novotná
Ken Pratt
Göran Radalewski
Julian Schneider
Orson Sieverding
York Stille
Stephan Thierbach
Susanne Titz
Ulrich Urban
Pia Witzmann
Leopold Wollenberger

Diese Publikation erscheint anlässlich der Ausstellung / This book is published in conjunction with the exhibition:

Pola Sieverding THE EPIC
NAK Neuer Aachener Kunstverein
3. April – 5. Juni 2016
April 3rd – June 5th 2016

Herausgeber / Editor:
NAK Neuer Aachener Kunstverein
Konzept / Concept: Pola Sieverding
Autoren / Authors: Maurice Funken, Ben Kaufmann, Michael Kohtes, Kirsten Maar
Gestaltung / Graphic design:
Ta-Trung, Berlin
Digital Mastering, Lithografie / Digital mastering, lithography: Orson Sieverding
Lektorat / Copyediting: Sylvia Zirden, Lance Anderson
Übersetzung / Translation:
Benjamin Letzler
Projektmanagement / Project management:
Constanze Korb, Hatje Cantz
Verlagsherstellung / Production:
Janine Lattich, Hatje Cantz
Druck und Bindung / Printing and binding:
DZA Druckerei zu Altenburg GmbH

Schrift / Typeface: Akzidenz Grotesk, Lyon
Papier / Paper: MultiOffset 170 g/m², MultiArt Gloss 200 g/m²

NAK Neuer Aachener Kunstverein
Vorstand / Executive Board: Dr. Werner Dohmen, Michael Heins, Prof. Dr. Doris Klee, Prof. Dr. Alexander Markschies, Sylvia Stille
Direktor / Director: Ben Kaufmann
Assistenz / Assistant: Maurice Funken

Erschienen im / Published by:
Hatje Cantz Verlag GmbH
Mommsenstraße 27, 10629 Berlin
Germany / Deutschland
Tel. +49 30 346 467 800
Fax +49 30 346 467 829
www.hatjecantz.com
Ein Unternehmen der Ganske Verlagsgruppe
A Ganske Publishing Group Company

Hatje Cantz books are available internationally at selected bookstores. For more information about our distribution partners, please visit our website at www.hatjecantz.com.

ISBN 978-3-7757-4412-6
Printed in Germany

Umschlagabbildung / Cover illustration:
The Epic, Videostill, 2016

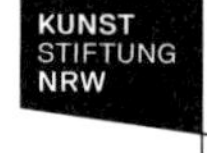

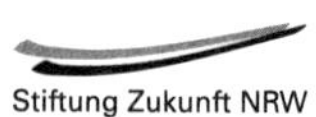

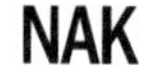